Madhavi Mahadevan has published two collections of short stories, *Paltan Tales* and *Doppelganger*, and an e-novella, *Swansong*. Her first novel, *The Kaunteyas*, was a retelling of the *Mahabharata* from the viewpoint of Kunti, the mother of the Pandavas. This was followed by *Bride of the Forest: The Untold Story of Yayati's Daughter*, which was also based on the *Mahabharata*, and told the story of Drishadvati, one of its lesser-known characters. She has also written fiction for children.

Praise for *Bride of the Forest: The Untold Story of Yayati's Daughter*

'A rich, pitch-perfect novel.' —Ashok Banker

'...a harrowing saga of grace about a woman who managed to be generous, kind and compassionate even while held hostage to the feckless notions of dharma adhered to by powerful men...The author does an admirable job of handling the sensational material with sensitivity even as she infuses it with the gentle beats of a pain-wracked heart.' —Anuja Chandramouli, *The New Indian Express*

'With lyrical prose, interesting characters and side characters and strong philosophical points, this book is a must-read.' —Times of India.Indiatimes.com

'In [*Bride of the Forest*], Drishadvati is a delicately poised figure while tracing feminist lineage...Mahadevan sensitively focuses on Drishadvati's radical character instead of projecting her as a helpless woman, as in earlier adaptations.' —*Hindustan Times*

Praise for *The Kaunteyas: Queen Kunti's Mahabharata*

'Kunti's fine characterisation is bound to touch readers.' — *The Hindu*

'Every chapter ends with a cliffhanger, the dialogues are realistic and there is no dead-air.' —*The New Indian Express*

'The book stands out for its fresh interpretation of the epic. Told as a first person narrative, the novel paints the character of Kunti as an intelligent, strong and thinking individual who stands up for herself to keep her place in society.' —*The Times of India*

The Forgotten Wife

The Story of HIDIMBI
and BHEEM

Madhavi Mahadevan

SPEAKING TIGER

SPEAKING TIGER BOOKS LLP
125 A, Shahpur Jat, New Delhi 110049

First published by Speaking Tiger Books in paperback in 2023

ISBN: 978-93-5447-604-4
eISBN: 978-93-5447-606-8

10 9 8 7 6 5 4 3 2 1

Typeset in Baskerville MT Std by SÜRYA, New Delhi
Printed at HT Media Ltd, Greater Noida

There is a capacity of virtue in us, and there is a capacity of vice to make your blood creep.

—Ralph Waldo Emerson

Do monsters really exist?
Surely they must, for if they did not, how could we?

—Jeffrey Jerome Cohen,
Monster Culture (Seven Theses)

Contents

1. The Burning 1
2. Kunti 4
3. Hidimba and Hidimbi 17
4. Our Lady of the Shala Trees 41
5. First Love 56
6. The Proposal 87
7. The Plan 101
8. A Mother's Wish 112
9. The Bride's Day 133
10. The Runaway Hours 149
11. The Unborn 157
12. Faultlines 163
13. Birth 179
14. Ghatotkach 201
15. Death Blow 217
16. Reunion 230

1

The Burning

The hour is appropriate for what has to be done. It is past midnight when the fire is lit. Engulfing the outhouse where the straw, hemp, bamboo and other building materials have been stored, it spreads to the main building. An angry beast with a thousand glowing tongues steadily licking the walls, it turns their home into an inferno. Dark acrid smoke swarms into the inner rooms.

As the jaws begin to close in, the five who wait by the opening of the underground tunnel are swamped by a sense of disbelief. Hissing softly, forking, racing and flying from wall to pillar to ceiling, the flames create a hellish brightness. The heat is unbearable. Despite the wet cloths wrapped around their faces, the foul-smelling smoke enters their lungs, sweat trickles down their limbs and tears blur their vision. There is a loud thud, the ground trembles. Somewhere close to them, a column has fallen.

For the past twelve months, the family living in the house has been leading a double life. They are on a sojourn; the lavishly decorated house is a gift from their relative Duryodhan. However, the guards around it have been placed not only for their safety but also to spy on them. Seemingly free, they are under a detention of sorts. Despite tipoffs about the diabolical plot meant to harm them, and despite making their own counterplot to escape, until this moment they had not fully grasped the extent of Duryodhan's treachery. The walls and this roof that had sheltered them had been designed solely as their funeral pyre. This was their dissolution.

In a few minutes, they would leave behind the comfort of everything known and familiar, enter the door of no return, and begin the descent into a deeper darkness. Till now they were known to the world as the Pandavas, sons of Pandu, erstwhile king of Hastinapur. The dream of attaining their father's kingdom was now out of their reach. Worse, their very existence had been snatched from them. Disappearing into the night, what skin will they wear tomorrow? Landless, homeless, powerless—by what name will they call themselves? Bereft of their identity, who will they claim as their ancestors and their gods? With the life they had known snatched away so cruelly, the only thing left to do was to keep body and soul together somehow, to stay as one.

Forewarned, they had prepared as best as they could for this situation. In the preceding months, they had revised their escape plan several times before settling on the safest route through the surrounding forest towards the river. It was their only chance. On the opposite bank lay uncharted territory, the country of the rakshasas—a place of chaos, magic and great danger.

Of course, we will not venture there unarmed, Bheem had stoutly declared more than once. But Yudhisthir had ruled against them carrying arms. By waiting until the last minute to do so, he hoped that the abruptness of his decision would shorten his brothers' anguish. If their ruse was to succeed at all they would have to leave their weapons behind, he said. Four pairs of eyes stared at him in total disbelief. Bheem without his mace? Arjun without his bow? 'All we need now, to complete the story of our extinction, is a begging bowl,' Bheem muttered in disgust. Yudhisthir reasoned with him: how else will we convince our enemies that we are dead? Among the five brothers, Bheem is the most intractable, but in the end he too complies. Of all the sacrifices they have had to make, abandoning their weapons is the most painful.

2

Kunti

For their mother Kunti, the past year in the house of lac had been a peculiar experience. Sensing the anger and anxiety in her sons, she had suffered silently with them. Her involvement in the day-to-day running of the household had kept her busy and had allowed her to conceal her fears.

However, since a few hours ago, when she recognised that the moment to act had come, an odd calmness has descended upon her, as if iced water had begun to flow in her veins. As if Time itself was regulating her actions—by reminding her of the past.

❖

On that fateful day many years ago, when she had found her husband Pandu lifeless on the floor of Shatashringa forest, Kunti had known that it was the death of her dreams too. At that moment the desire to live had deserted her. But Madri, the younger co-wife, had pleaded through a veil of tears: '*I* want to go with him, Sister. I just don't have it in me to live a life without him. Among us three, you have always been the most sensible. You will be a better mother to my two boys than I can ever be. Not only that, you will take the place of their father too, and ensure that they are not deprived of their rightful position in the world. Unlike you, I lack that clarity of knowing what needs to be done at the right moment.'

What needs to be done. No one had taught her, but Kunti had somehow always known how to do it. She had acquired the nerve—as cold, pointed and unyielding as a fine steel blade—for it.

A shadow resides in her heart: it will never leave. Though invisible to the world, in her troubled moments, it reveals parts of itself, as if to assert its hold on her. She believes that the demon she has always found herself pitted against is Providence itself and she has already lost far too much to it. The long, sleepless nights in this house had strengthened her conviction that the walls were relentlessly closing in on her—again. If she had to protect herself and her sons, she must depend on no one and nothing but her own wits. But hadn't it always been so? Didn't she learn very early what it meant to be vulnerable even when one is seemingly protected by one's family?

She was still in her infancy when her father, the Vrishni chieftain Shura, had passed her on to his cousin and close friend, Kuntibhoj, who was then childless. Torn from her mother's arms and thrust into those of strangers, she had been left to cope with a grief that she was too young to comprehend: the pain of being abandoned. Consequently, she had felt it more deeply.

Years later, when she was an adolescent, in a manner that was almost as cavalier as Shura's, her foster father had placed her in the service of the visiting sage, Durvasa. Dreaded in all Aryavarta for his short temper and whimsicality, Durvasa was known to be a particularly difficult guest. Yet, Kunti had served him with complete devotion, putting up with his quirks and demands stoically while striving to please, because that, she had been told, was what was expected of her. Her own feelings, she understood implicitly, were of no importance. The year in Durvasa's service and the subsequent one, too, were the most distressing time in her young life. Having no one to confide in had deepened her sense of isolation.

Later, the marriage to Pandu, king of Hastinapur and scion of an ancient line, had brought a change in her fortunes, but it failed to give her the happiness she had hoped for. Their incapacity to have children together was the reason. An added cause of her sadness was that Pandu, at the urging of the Kuru family elders, had taken a second wife. Putting on a brave face, Kunti had welcomed the new bride, Madri, although it had left her feeling even more lonesome. She had loved her husband intensely, but indulging her emotions had never been easy for her. Their relationship, toeing the line of orthodoxy, had been affable rather than passionate. A part of her had thus remained independent of him. Pandu, too, had realised at a deeper level that Madri, pretty Madri, who knew how to charm and vied openly for his love, was more vulnerable than the level-headed chief queen.

This knowledge had engendered in him a special fondness for his second wife.

Following his death and Madri's suicide, Kunti had finally understood that abandonment was, in fact, the leitmotif of her life. However, she had not allowed herself the luxury of bemoaning her fate or even grieving. She had to worry about her own and the Pandavas' future. She was aware that all the dreams that Pandu and she had shared for their boys would turn to ashes unless she did something to salvage them. She had returned to her husband's kingdom nearly seventeen years after she had left it.

As expected, the Kauravas were sympathetic and welcoming towards the widowed queen. They had made space for her and her boys under the ancestral roof and treated them well. But her brother-in-law Dhritarashtra's sons, particularly Duryodhan, who as the eldest was accustomed to running his writ in Hastinapur, had resented the Pandavas. The incipient rivalry between the cousins made Kunti realise, early enough, that ensuring that Pandu's sons would not be deprived of their patrimony was not going to be a simple matter. She had also understood that she would have to summon up a new spirit, a very different one from what had been required of her as Pandu's wife and then as his widow, if they were to survive.

The twelve months they had endured in the house of lac had sharpened her instincts. Thus, when the chance to escape had come, quite unexpectedly, she had simply seized it.

❖

The servants had left for the day when the tribal woman and her five sons appeared at her door. Was it just a coincidence that they had come to the house at precisely that hour? She had never seen them before. Why had they come? From where? Had they hitched a ride on the wind? The western sky was overcast. The rising dust particles clogging the air foretold a storm. Indeed, the family of six, so dark and silent, seemed to have materialised out of that swirling dust and the drifting detritus. The mother gaunt, the sons lean to the point of emaciation.

There was always some food left over in the kitchen, even after the servants had eaten. Kunti had invited the family to eat. As she served them the meal in the passage outside the kitchen, she had to steady her trembling hand and school herself not to look at their faces, not see those six pairs of identical dark eyes quick, darting and birdlike. Though avoiding eye contact had made it a bit easier, there had been a brief moment when the youngest of the five sons had asked her for a second helping of something. He had looked directly at her.

His eyes were the colour of rain-washed earth. They presaged a greening, a coming of age, yet they were curiously defenceless. How old was he? Fourteen or fifteen, no more...limbs still growing, sparse hair just beginning to sprout on his face, in which a childlike softness still lingered. He was the most friendly among them, the one who had earlier shyly offered her a comb of forest honey. Like the others, he too had tried to keep a poker face, but when she had served him a cup of payesh, a smile had broken through, like a shaft of sunbeam through pale grey clouds.

Seeing that clean, candid smile, her resolve had nearly crumbled. However, she had retained her wits long enough to calmly suggest to the woman and her sons that they should stay the night as there was a thunderstorm brewing. Liquor followed by comfortable beds would ensure a sound sleep for them. Tomorrow, she'd added as the final cajolery, they would have to do a slew of simple chores—in return for grain. Unsuspecting, they had taken up the offer with alacrity.

Don't think about it. Drunk and asleep, they will not know anything. No struggle. It would have been quick…and over by now.

Yet, she finds herself praying. But the approaching flames show her no mercy.

It is as if the fire has been a witness all along and now the flames bring to light the madness of her life in a vivid montage of scenes that have been caged in the eternal darkness where one's worst demons go. Sorrow, guilt, shame and the nastiest of all, helplessness, rise to torment her, to remind her that it is *she* who is the caged one, and all her rationalisations are bereft of meaning. Who would believe in her innocence? A single indiscretion in her youth, whose actual details are now hazy, has brought her a lifetime's worth of secret shame. She is powerless, as she has always been.

She knows how she will be judged if ever it were to become known that she was an unwed mother. Who would understand that she had been just fifteen then?

That she had acted with the foolish impetuosity of the young. The smear on her reputation will be transferred to the Pandavas, ruining their lives forever. They too will *never* understand, never trust her again. She will lose their respect. No, her secret must remain forever swaddled in silence.

After this night has passed, she will not recall all the details of the terrible tableaux of remembering that is playing out in her mind as the fire edges closer. But she will never forget two scenes, of extraordinary clarity, that are inexorably closing the circle around her. The first: a fifteen-year-old girl setting a cradle on the river's current, weeping copiously while heaping benedictions on the newborn babe sleeping inside. The next, separated by almost three decades: an older version of the same mother, dry-eyed, silent, trembling, a terrified watcher as the son born out of wedlock and long abandoned stands resurrected before her.

But who is he, this unknown archer who dares to enter uninvited the vast arena of kshatriya princes? Around her, in the royal enclosure and its vicinity, the murmurs of protest swell among the spectators as someone recognises the imposter and asks: what is a charioteer's son doing here? From where does he get the impunity to challenge the incomparable Arjun to a contest?

Ignoring the ridicule, with pride embedded in every line of his body and etched in the stiff, unrelenting mask of his face, the trespasser looks as ominous and baleful as a mighty tusker. In his bearing there is defiance and audacity, but also, strangely, the vulnerability of a mortal. Meanwhile, the cheers rise from the citizens packed in the galleries on the opposite side of the arena. *Karna, Karna, Karna.*

She recognises him instantly. Mortification, dread, guilt and something else—an inexplicable sunburst of joy—shatters her heart to pieces. A miracle. *He is alive! My son is alive.* While everyone else witnessing the scene in the arena sees a man of humble birth, she alone recognises him for who he is: her firstborn. The eldest Kaunteya. Seeing his golden earrings, a gift from his divine father Surya, she is reminded of the prediction that had been made for him, of a glorious destiny. Had he come to claim it? As the crowds identify in him an archer who is one of them, they cheer to the skies. Meanwhile, there is anger and dismay among the aristocrats who sense a shake-up in the societal order they have developed over generations. And Kunti, too, has her awakening in a moment of complete, terrifying lucidity.

See what you have done to me, Mother. Pranadayini. Giver of Life. Witness the life of humiliation that you *gave me. Bear your guilt forever. Understand that in* this *world a mother's crime cannot go unpunished.*

Time shows its pitiless face, returning to Kunti the poisoned fruit that is hers alone. She sees for herself a harsh justice. *Son. Brother. Enemy.* Though he is alive, she can never accept Karna as her firstborn son. Not after all that has happened. Not now when so much is at stake. She cannot jeopardise the claim of Yudhisthir, the eldest Pandava, to the throne of Hastinapur. Meanwhile, in a dramatic turn of events unfolding in the arena, Karna and Arjun are caught in the grip of an implacable rivalry. In the future, it will demand from her, their mother, an impossible choice: which one of them will live and which one will die.

❖

Staring at the approaching flames now, she understands that there is going to be no liberation from her secret. As in the past, it has placed her once more at a crossroads. This burning, it is she who is responsible. It was *she* who had, unwittingly, lit the first match—a lifetime ago. It is *she* who must see it through. The family of six who had come to her door a few hours earlier were innocent, trusting folk, hoping only for the gift of food. Absorbed in convincing them to stay the night, she had not even bothered to ask them their names. But now their faces rise in front of her eyes, every single one, floating towards her through the encroaching flames. Their stares cling to her, wide open with horror, questioning, accusing, before slowly turning inward, as they breathe one last time. The light in those eyes swallowed by a final darkness. A tunnel with no end. Their doom led them to her, but it is she who has decided that they must die—and arranged for it.

Is that all we were to you—just kindling? Was there no room for compassion in your heart for us?

Overwhelmed by a wave of anxiety, she feels dizzy and unsteady on her feet.

'Mother, you cannot remain here any longer.' Yudhisthir's eyes bear down on her, his voice sharp with concern.

'Where are your brothers?' She is surprised at how calm she sounds.

'Arjun, Nakul and Sahadev are inside the tunnel. You, too, must join them without delay.'

She shakes her head. 'I started it...I sent him—my son—'

'We are not leaving without Bheem.' Yudhisthir's manner is calm and reassuring. 'I'll wait for him, Mother. He should be here any moment. Please go in.'

His words jerk her back to the present. Though he is trying to hide it from her, she senses the same panic in him that is twisting in her gut. The silent screams rising higher than the flames—is it her imagination? Where are they coming from? Is it a cry for help? Has something gone terribly wrong at the last minute? She has tried to be composed, but the thought of losing her son unravels her. What is taking him so long? Can any living creature pass through that wall of fire unscathed? For all his incredible strength, he is not immortal. Bheem, the middle son. Though physically the strongest of the Pandavas, he has always been overshadowed by his elder brother Yudhisthir's shining intellect on the one hand and by Arjun's unmatched military prowess on the other. She too has tended to treat him more like an impetuous, reckless, hot-tempered child who is a little too ready with his fists. Of all her sons, he worries her the most. What if he too—without him there is nothing ahead. Nothing but these insatiable flames. She lunges towards the fire.

'Mother!' Yudhisthir tries to restrain her physically. 'Get inside the tunnel with the others.'

But she is past listening or caring. A fresh wave of despair overcomes her. 'Can't you hear the screams? How can you not? They are deafening. Maybe he could not leave them. You know him! Go, help him. I will not—' Undone by her panic, she begs for her son's life. 'Save your brother! We cannot leave him behind. You cannot let him die. He is ours, do you not understand? *Ours!*'

Yudhisthir is taken aback. His mother is not given to emotional excitement; he has never even seen her weep. Yet here she is, babbling incoherently, wide-eyed in fright. 'Bheem knows how to take care of himself, Mother,' he says. 'He should be here any moment.'

Suddenly he appears. At first an inchoate gigantic shape, golden-hued. A rush of manic energy. A magnificent chthonic being, half human half beast, made of glowing dust that coalesces into a mighty form hurtling through the flames. As if the fire has forged a new supernatural version of a human. An indestructible weapon, that body. Made taller by anger. War-like. A fury bent on devastation. The face contorted in a snarl. A monstrous death mask. A deep, chilling bellow emerges from him as if this exalted image, at last, is the true self revealed. Not the sacrifice, not the sacrificer, he is the god himself. A savage, intoxicated, vengeful god. A god who will restore, but only after a thorough cleansing: by burning down all that needs to be destroyed. The goal of this birth is destruction.

It is an image of Bheem that she will never forget.

3

Hidimba and Hidimbi

It is the fourteenth night of the waning moon. At an unholy hour, an orange red incandescence breaks the darkness outside the settlement of Varnavat. A pillar of fire grows into the sky. An untimely wind rises like a new evil, sweeping the sparks from the burning house over the low perimeter wall towards a palash forest. Furious red tongues snap to life everywhere. Like a conquering army, the firestorm ravages the forest.

Among the wild creatures, the swift-footed, like the chital, manage to outrun it; the pangolins, porcupines and mongooses go deeper inside their underground lairs; the mynas, sparrows and rose-ringed parakeets rise and scatter in all directions. But it is the nesting season. Gone without a struggle are the young ones: the embryos, the naked and sightless hatchlings. As a fine glaze over the stench of burning flesh, the malevolent wind carries the quiet surrender of their tender breaths.

❖

A few hours later, in a different forest, a young woman gazes at the sky where the birds have been in a frenzy all night. Their thin, disjointed cries have fallen to a slow, steady dirge, telling of the horrors they have witnessed and mourning the loss of their babies. But now, as the first light tiptoes in, they are nearly all gone. The only reminder of their grief is the unsettling hush and, in the distance, a low hanging blue-grey cloud, a sombre pennant veiling the rosiness of dawn.

'That's smoke,' her brother says, a hard edge to his voice. 'They are burning. Again.'

She does not ask who 'they' are. She knows that he will not deign to reply. Older by several years, Hidimba acknowledges her presence only when he has a use for her. Something tells her that this is going to be one of those times. A sign: his nose is twitching.

Reddish and misshapen from a fight in his youth, it looks like a yam embedded in the centre of his bloated, hairy face, a monstrosity. But its sense of smell is stronger than that of an elephant. He turns his head to the left and right, sniffs the air several times, then shuts his eyes to discern better the shapes of the new odours that he has detected. 'Coming towards us. Humans. Several full-grown males. Four or more.' His nose twitches in annoyance. 'Hmm…never seen a human move so fast. Like a hurricane.' He frowns and sniffs the air again. 'Yes, definitely human males, *but*…there is a faint scent of a female too.'

'A woman? Surely not! Are these people—'

'Arya,' he says forcefully. He spits on the ground to show his irritation, disgust and contempt.

'But their women never come this way,' she says, frowning. 'They wouldn't dare. They know that this is our…rakshasa territory.'

After a moment he lifts his head, sniffs the air again and sends her a slow, pleased smile. 'They do smell strongly of fear.'

Her stomach clenches. He is her only sibling, but lately she has begun to feel that she detests him.

❖

Fists have always been his first resort and reason the last. While belligerence is a trait valued among their kind, Hidimba has developed an excess of it. As the firstborn of the rakshasi queen Hariti, he sees himself as the overall leader of all the different tribes in the forest. However, a deep, inflexible hostility—brooding and atavistic—lurks within. Revealing itself in the aggression of the protruding lower jaw, the cold distrust in his sly, upward slanting eyes, the battle lines permanently knitted on his sloping brow, it warns others to give him a wide berth. The old-timers say that it is the result of a miscegenation: a quick, slick sexual encounter between a pishacha and a rakshasi. A double whammy, they call it, for the world at large.

Pilupala, the pishacha who fathered him, was a homeless delinquent who appeared out of the blue one fine day. On the edge of the forest, at a fork in the road there was a silk-cotton tree. He would hang out there. The road lay alongside a burial ground, which was the favoured haunt of an assorted gang of bhutas, pretas and vetalas—ghosts and reanimated corpses—who shared a camaraderie and called themselves the Tamasiks. These itinerant spirits were a boisterous lot. Their lifestyle was clearly not for the faint-hearted.

The Tamasiks considered ordinary practices like wearing clothes abhorrent. They revered Mahakaal, the destroyer, and Kali, the dark goddess of death; they drank to these deities from cups made of human skulls. The crania of the vilest criminals were prized for the subtle flavours distilled from heinous sins. They lent, the Tamasiks claimed, a piquancy to the liquor. Other pursuits involved assuming bizarre forms—such as the headless horseman, the old crone with her feet pointing backwards—and frightening to death travellers who had wandered off the highway, muttering incantations that caused skeletons to rise from their graves and flail their bones in a monstrous dance, directing dark streams of horrible nightmares to those lying down for a hard-earned sleep, possessing the weak-minded and speaking through their mouths in the sepulchral tongues of their dead ancestors who would demand pinda, the cooked rice balls studded with black sesame seeds, their favourite funeral food.

As pishachas went, Pilupala was the most vicious kind, a rakt pishacha, addicted to drinking blood. Come nightfall, he would shake off the lassitude that daylight caused in him, clamber out of the bole of the silk-cotton tree and slope off in the direction of the villages where livestock had been shut for the night. Pigs, dogs, goats, sheep, cows, donkeys, horses…when it came to blood-drinking, his tastes were eclectic. But what he prized as the most energising drink was a certain kind of human blood. Young, well-built men were the best source. His search for the right donors had left a trail of pale-faced youth who, from being in the flush of good health and vigour, would begin to weaken day by day, regressing into morose shadows that lay curled up in gloomy corners, wanting only to be left alone. Their worried families would call in a powerful tantrik who would immediately smell out the presence of a pishacha and spell out the prescribed remedies—for a fee. Thus, door after door would be barred and Pilupala would have to go even further afield in search of fresh blood.

The addiction to blood had spawned in him another curious interest, indeed, a marrow-deep passion, for genealogy. Every drop of blood tasted by his tongue betrayed a long and crooked story of the victim's powers, passions and weaknesses. He was fascinated by the patterns these stories revealed. To anyone who cared to listen, he would brag about the antiquity of his own bloodline. He claimed that Krodha, one of the thirteen daughters of Prajapati Daksha, the son of Brahma, was his progenitrix. Like all her sisters, she was married off to the powerful sage Kashyap. Like them, she too was remarkably fecund, but what set her apart from the rest was a particularly vile temper—that *all* her descendants had inherited.

The other members of the Tamasiks privately thought that Pilupala had a tendency to theatrics because it allowed him to make much of his physical attributes. The look he loved to show off—bulging veins, purple-red eyes and clenched jawline—could get tedious and even a bit absurd. But his willingness to do stuff they backed away from, such as seducing and impregnating sleeping women, consuming dead bodies and sucking the blood of an infant still in its mother's womb, made him a daredevil of sorts.

Pilupala's reputation was dodgy, dangerous, but also enticing. It attracted some of the younger female rakshasis who used to visit the burial grounds for a lark and a quiet smoke of ganja. Among them, Hariti, then an impressionable teen and not yet the queen, was the most enamoured with him. His lean dark looks, the mean scowl, the thick long ponytail and that way he had of leering, which sent delightful shivers down her spine, were the silken threads of his charm that drew her to him. She yearned to know what he saw when he looked at her and what he thought of her. She dared to speculate about what all he might do to her if they were ever alone. One moonless night, she decided to find out.

A misadventure, her family elders called it, shaking their heads in dismay. They asked, couldn't she have chosen someone a bit more steady like a daitya or even a yaksha as her first lover? Look at the grief the misbegotten fellow had brought upon her! Pishachas were at least three rungs lower in the social hierarchy than rakshasas. All those stories about coming from Brahma's golden egg were just that—imaginative yarns. Pishachas came from an unknown source, maybe it was just the debris floating from some planet in outer space that had brought this nasty germ to their part of the world. It turned out that Pilupala, in that first and last encounter with Hariti, had, out of sheer habit than any real desire, dug his fangs a bit too deep into her jugular vein, leading to a copious loss of blood before she had managed to unfasten his grip and fling him off with all her considerable strength. She was sore, her skin was scratched and carried the deadly puncture marks, she looked washed out. But she was unrepentant. It had been merely a temporary crush, she said. As natural as growing up. Her tone was a mix of sheepishness, defiance and nonchalance.

Soon after the mating, Pilupala, to everyone's relief, took off for some unknown destination. He was never seen or heard of again. Meanwhile, Hariti, too preoccupied with morning sickness, didn't mourn his departure. Hidimba's birth was preceded by terrible omens—the baying of hyenas, the appearance of spectres, cases of spontaneous combustion—but the rakshasas, a rapidly dying breed, celebrated it with their customary gusto.

❖

A few years after the pishacha Pilupala's disappearance, Hariti had found love again. True love. And Hidimba's half-sister entered the world. Everyone wondered how the elder sibling would react to the newborn.

On being presented with the little bundle of joy, his first thought, typically, was to test if this wriggling piece of baby flesh was as tasty as it looked. Fortunately, the same midwife who had supervised his entry into the world was in attendance on Hariti for this birthing too. The woman remembered, just in time, that when she had held him upside down and smacked his bottom, instead of responding with a wail, Hidimba had clamped her forearm firmly between his jaws. The embryonic pointed teeth, a distinct pishacha trait, had left a row of permanent indentations in her skin that she sometimes showed off. Recognising that fiendish gleam of old in his eyes, she intervened before he could sink his sharp incisors into the baby. In retaliation, Hidimba snatched the bundle from her and flung it aside. It sailed into a bed of stinging nettle. Everyone expected a howl of some sort from the little rakshasi—pain, protest, outrage or an avowal of revenge would have been typical of her kind—but the babe merely kicked her legs and gave a wide smile. In sheer relief, they laughed.

To their great astonishment, they saw Hidimba unfurrow his brow and stare at his half-sister intently. After a moment, he too laughed. It was a first for him, they said, recognising that a firewall had, miraculously, been breached. However, it took a while for him to understand that his sister was a playmate, and not a plaything. Throwing-the-Baby was his favourite sport for a few days, but rakshasas, like all forest-dwellers, are hardwired for a rough life from infancy and she survived the drops from tree-tops. In fact, she developed a head for heights and a deep love for trees. Her mother built her a tree-house on a shala tree and the little girl was named Shalakatankati, the girl who lived on the shala tree.

Unruffled by his cheerless demeanour and overall boorishness, Hidimba's little sister followed him everywhere. So hardy and tireless a companion was she that she even took to answering to his name. Hidimba, an eerie hollow-sounding name meaning nothing, had somehow defined him. Now it took on a lilting, lighter adjunct: Hidimba-Hidimbi was how the siblings came to be known. Their patch of forest was called Hidimbavan.

Like him, she grew up tall, sinewy and strong, but unlike him she had a moderate temper and a friendly disposition. Everyone attributed this difference in their temperaments to the fact that the siblings did not share the same father. Hidimbi's birth father was a gandharva, a suave celestial musician, who had strayed into the forest and charmed Hariti with his divine looks as much as he had becalmed her stormy nature with his honeyed lyrics and soothing airs. Their romance was deep and tender. Sadly, it too was short-lived.

❖

Now, the adolescent Hidimbi is a picture of feminine loveliness. She has also developed a new poise that stands at odds with her brother's aggression. Hidimbi is the harmony to Hidimba's discord, the rainbow to his storminess, the gentle balm to the blows he inflicts with unholy gusto on others.

Ferociousness, though pronounced in Hidimba, is merely a trait that comes in a bouquet of other unlovely rakshasa traits: a slavering mouth, thick, unkempt hair, coppery skin, yellow glowing eyes and pointed ears. Eight prominent curved fangs embellish his dental display. In addition, he is blessed with one peculiarity, a supernatural sense of smell. Odours that are to lesser noses simply normal and nice, or unfamiliar and unpleasant, are to him the essence of this living earth. Embraced joyously by his snout, they are the long-lost prodigal children who have miraculously found their way back to the ancestral home. Entering his wide nostrils en masse, they are the language of secrets. An inventory of desires and depravities, they reveal the fundamental nature of all the living forms that had originally emerged from the long rope of breath with which Prajapati Brahma had seeded Time and Space.

Hidimba's nose knows, for instance, from the faintest ferrous whiff when the tiniest drop of blood is shed, what kind of creature the blood comes from. It senses the wet skin of earthworms and when a tree's roots are dying. It tells the time by the odours of the hour. The forest's amalgam of scents changes by the minute. Dawn, free of sin, shot with soft-hued colours is a demure bride lifting a fine veil and looking up with wide, kohl-rimmed eyes. Enmeshed in the threads of her finery is the glitter of bird calls. She brings with her the fresh, delicate fragrance of possibilities: of new blooms unfurling, of snails waking up, of gold oozing gently from honeycombs, of sweet sap rising along stems like a soul-force. The feel-good scent lingers till noon which is the rush hour of sharp, lurid tangs—animal poop, bird droppings, a kill half-devoured, overripe mangoes and jackfruit splashed messily on the forest floor, nectar slowly souring, gases rising from dark brown swampy patches. By dusk, most life smells the same. It has turned stale, begun to disintegrate and stinks of rot. It is ready to be consigned to the pyres lighting up the western sky.

Among all these hours—and the odours they supply—twilight is Hidimba's finest hour. It is the time when he, like all rakshasas, feels energised and ready to reconnect with the wider world in a deeper, more meaningful way. Gaining in vitality, his senses come preternaturally alive, preparing for an unusual spray of odours, the midnight scent of dreams.

At that bewitched hour, the Self within casts aside its veil and projects the lusts born of ignorance. Untethered by deep sleep, with the senses lying at rest, every last desire, dread and discontent that is born in the three worlds steps out of the body. The deliria form a lively, strutting parade that ranges through the boundless night, singing, tweeting, chirruping, free like the luminous fireflies that flit seductively from grass to bush to tree branch, now on, now off. Delusions, being naturally promiscuous, hook up at random. The motley dream-chain grows by borrowing bits of other desires that are mismatched individually but stitched together make a sly, elusive sense called Life. Even as it begins, the thread begins to disintegrate and return to dust, but everywhere the phantasmagoria wanders, it leaves lingering traces of its fleshly origins—in aromas that the rakshasa's eager, quivering nose picks up as if they are scented love notes. A night-wanderer by nature, Hidimba stalks the dream odours, collecting them as a boy might pick pebbles on a riverbank, some smooth, others irregular, no two exactly alike, but all a part of his prized collection: lovers' dreams of fire on fire, the slowing thrum of sated desire; piscine dreams soggy with a lonely, decaying passion; the sad musk of unrequited love; just-born dreams smelling of amniotic fluid; bloodthirsty sharp-toothed shards of dreams betrayed; grotesque half-formed aborted dreams; dizzying dreams of perfection; powdery dreams of disenchantments and epiphanies blunted by time; enigmatic last and final dreams that, nevertheless, hint at a sequel. There are also the haunting pop-ups of zombie dreams—the spectres of desires denied a proper burial.

In the nocturnal forest of delusions, in its opacity, he feels a sense of comfort that daylight and the commonplace world denies him. He discovers both a pathos and an opulence, fragmentation and wholeness. Death and continuity. The real struggle of a life lies not in its birth chart but in its combination of desires, in the vastness of its dreams, their tenacity to grow out of nothing, to become a tissue of entanglements, a battlefield rife with obstacles. Here, demons and demon-slayers, like night and day, are perennially coupled in the same spinning dance.

However, he dreads the dreams of the long-dead. Coming night after night to haunt him, these are the conversations among the inconsolable, the defeated, the homeless, the lost. Heartbreak and grief, the salt of tears mingled with the tartness of rage, the sourness of regret, the vitriol of revenge denied. How did we fail? Why? Didn't we do enough to preserve what we had, save it for our children? Our deities crushed, our homes and humble possessions smashed into the earth, our cities desolated and burial grounds flooded, our sleeping dead rising in a flotilla of welcome for those whose lives had gone up in smoke. Our dead, our dead, our dead. How do we count their numbers? Who will account for their untimely end, their unlived years that hang like millstones around our necks?

Night marchers everywhere, the spectres of dead men tell him their chilling tales: we fought but we failed to protect. We fled from our lives *for* our lives. We died to our earlier existence in order to exist, to survive somehow, even if it was only as exiles moving in a slow shuffle towards a counterfeit being. Denied claim to the land of our ancestors, bereft of their language and their ways, who are we now but the derecognised? The unwashed who wash up in the greyness of a foreign land to a different tyranny. A place where kindness fades from faces the minute they see us; nourishment is withdrawn and babies grow quiet for so long that they are no longer babies any more but still, dead things to be wrapped in white bundles and left forever in the ground. Mothers weep in their dreams, fathers gnash their teeth. Nobody ever forgets. Stories wither in our hearts and songs dry up on our lips because no one can dredge up any longer the right words for either obituaries or dirge. Moving on and onward, homeward but never arriving, never reclaiming that elusive homeland, that lost glory. Food stolen or foraged and cooked under an indifferent sky. We breed—how can we not?—passing on our sorrow to our children. They inherit our silences, our emptiness, our death drive. They carry forth the hunched shoulders and the unseeing gaze that says I Do Not Exist. I Am Not There.

❖

'Terror gives a spicy kick to the prey's meat,' he says. 'They are running to save their skins.' The casualness of his tone does not deceive Hidimbi, nor does the almost benign smile hide the cruel glitter in his eyes. She understands that it isn't a joke but a guarantee. 'Expect them in a few hours.'

'If they are fleeing from some terrible danger themselves, they cannot threaten us,' she says in what she hopes is a neutral, reasonable tone. 'Can't we just ignore them?'

'*Ignore them?*' His nose jerks suddenly, in revulsion.

'When they can do us no harm then why kill them? Why not just let them be? They may only be passing through. Let them carry on.'

'*They are our mortal enemies*,' he says with a cold, deliberate emphasis. Suddenly he smiles, in a cruel parody of her gentleness. '*What* is wrong with you?' he asks in a voice tinged with woe. '*Why* can't you believe what you are told?'

Because I don't know you, she wants to say. You are not the same person anymore. We live in the same world but we no longer see it the same way. There is no comforting resonance between us. No warmth either. It was there once and it lent a certain simple joy to life. We played together. You showed me the jungle, its secret places. You taught me to climb trees, swim and fight. Be strong, you said. You and I are protectors. Our pura, you called this forest fortress. I understood your fierce loyalty to this mother soil that sustains us, your desire to guard it with your life—and admired you for it. I even wanted to be like you because I thought that as her inheritor you would be like our mother, strong but kind and just, wise but open and truthful. However, now your eyes tell me that there are secrets behind their gaze. I get the feeling that someone else lives inside your skin. The cool, level scrutiny is yours, but behind it lies an appraisal, a proprietorship that makes me uncomfortable. I sense a new pitilessness in you. But there are also times when I sense nothing, as if the mirror has broken. There is nothing left to see. No me. No one familiar inside, but this living, breathing void where something ugly and dangerous lies in wait, like a rabid animal licking a festering sore. You alarm me. This stranger you have become. This growing distrust of me. This nameless dread I have begun to feel whenever I am near you. Waiting, watching, nosing out my thoughts. I know you can read them. *I will have to do something about you, but what?*

'You must learn to have faith in me,' Hidimba says, his voice turning viscous, as if reasoning with a recalcitrant child. 'Killing an Arya is easier than you imagine. *They* have done it—even killed each other—in the past. Countless times.'

'Couldn't last night's burning have been an accident? Fire is not...'

'...evil in itself,' he finishes the sentence on a hardening note. An old routine between them, this ease with which he completes her sentences as if everything about her, even words, are his by right. 'Instead, those who use it as a weapon are evil.'

'But...'

Overriding her protest, he continues, 'Have you ever asked yourself how the kingdoms of Aryavarta have grown? I will tell you: with fires, floods, chariots, but above all, superior arms. Magical weapons—chakras, maces, vajras, axes, spears, bows and arrows and even mantras—that they obtain from the gods. There is no end to how much of this earth their kings want. It is not a custodianship for them, it is a possession. This soil which supports all our lives is a possession to be snatched and parcelled into neat little fields—for their use alone. The trees that exchange their breath with us are to be felled and burned. The waters that keep us green are harnessed for their prosperity alone. Once we were everywhere, our cities were unrivalled, but now we are limited to the little patches like this forest that will disappear because we failed to protect it. Isn't it better to die doing what one is born to do than become something else? When did you last hear of a rakshasa peacefully passing away of old age surrounded by a loving family? Our race has reached its end, fighting kshatriyas in wars or being destroyed in a grand rakshasa sacrifice by a powerful brahmin sage like Parashara. They hate us with a vengeance. Did you know that they boast about killing a rakshasa? It is a blood sport for them. We should be flattered that they respect our brute strength and tenacity enough to consider us as the most formidable of adversaries, but it's *they* who have the edge of superior weapons and newer skills. Our supernatural powers are merely a manifestation of our physical capability, but they have something far more deadly. Guile. In the end, they always defeat us, to our enduring shame. They increase their possessions while we, in our own land, become the refugees, the outsiders, the oppressed. They take our land and our basic rights. They break our spirit. They look down on us as savages and mock our speech to show how much more superior to us they are. They have invented a word for people like us who lack their refinement. We are anarya. It means we are uncivilised and unwelcome in Aryavarta. Do you know how many of us—danavas, daityas, nagas, yakshas, gandharvas, rakshasas, pishachas, kiratas, nishadhas, khasas—have died at their hands fighting to preserve a space of our own? Among themselves, they have several different classes, but when it comes to us, there is only one desirable class: the dead. Extinct. When you are nothing more than a dangerous animal for them to kill or subdue into service, why would you think of them as anything other than your enemy? When they make no effort to, at least understand us, why do you speak of kindness to them? They are not just our enemies, they conduct a war on life itself. It cannot be that this earth, its riches, belong to them alone...We have to keep them out. Bakasura *rules* the forest near Ekachakra because he has built a reputation for killing and eating humans. They are calling him Asuraraj nowadays. He does a wonderful mimicry of a brahmin simultaneously praying to his devatas and pleading to a rakshasa to spare his life.'

Hidimba cringes, brings his palms together. In a

hideous lampoon of terror and submission, he rolls his eyes wildly and stammers, 'Bhhh...bhhh...bhhh.' Suddenly he stops and smiles—the same mischievous, boyish grin of old—as if enjoying the look of frightened revulsion on her face.

Her mouth is dry. 'Baka was always a bit weird,' she says. 'I don't know why you are so friendly with him now. You used to thrash him at wrestling, remember? Every time he saw you, *he* would begin to stammer and shake like a leaf. How we used to make fun of him!' She sends him a half smile, hoping he will return it. Surely those memories of a happier time exist in him too, as they do in her. But the flash of annoyance in his eyes tells her it is not so. His loyalties have changed.

❖

Baka and his relatives, Kirmira, Alambusha and Alayudha, are Hidimba's new brotherhood. Arya sacrifices and the sages who perform the rituals are their pet hates. The rakshasas band together and go on a rampage whenever they hear that a yagna is being performed or a rishi is building a hermitage in the forest. Like him, they too are haunted by ghosts from the past and the questions they raise: what is more important—to keep a race alive or to save a way of life? To cremate an identity or to take a different one. To fade from memory as a language lost or to be reborn in a hybrid tongue? To cut off one's head, drive a stake through one's heart or to promise a comeback. To avenge or not. It is the only strength left to them, the descendants of the vanquished and the exiled, the captives and the runaways, this urge to dream backwards. Hidimba's head buzzes with those unsettling dreams. The bereavement and the suppressed anger in them spark off an incandescence in him. *We were too arrogant. We didn't do enough.* A war cry rises in his soul.

We protect. We resist. We destroy.

Then comes the menacing prospect of fury bloodshot with vengeance, a twisting lava flow overhung by a cloud of pride, inexorable anger and a corrosive guilt. Pursuits down dark, curving paths that only seem to go backwards. Guts knotted tight, cold sweat, heartbeats pounding the pavements of eternity, blood thundering faster than thought. The prey magically turns into the stalker. The gap thins to a bare hair's breadth. In the last wild ambush, the snarls and desperate cries commingle in one savage death song at the heart of which lies the same thing—a passion, an intense longing to taste the lifeblood of the soul. To be reborn as retribution. Within death lies immortality. The desire to kill is inseparable from the desire to die. In that confluence of desires, waiting, is the shining vision of an honourable death. The only meaningful death for a man. Hidimba is drunk on those dreams of glory, on their dark bloodlust. The smell of fear is an aphrodisiac, rich with promise; this poison in his blood, this malfeasance, this dream of vengeance. Like the asura fire in Patala that is perennially fed by water, this dream too is a fire, nourished by blood.

Blood. Iron. Its radiance a bubbling warmth on his palate. Its sheer variety: the shining energy in snake blood, the cold blue sting of scorpion blood, the hard punch of bat blood. And now human blood. Sweeter than mother's milk, richer than honey, more seductive than wine. It is the finest of foods for the ancestral deities who demand a bali, a sacrifice, before they grant a growth in supernatural powers. A human, too, is a sacrifice—the highest. A quick clean blow to break the neck or skull; the chest torn open; the warm ruby stream offered as a libation to the thirsting spirits. A reparation to satisfy the ancestors. A promise that when the time comes for the world to end, the red-hot flow contained within his veins will spill over and engulf every living thing. Only then, when the sinful are destroyed and the vanquished rise, shall the original gods, too, rise again.

❖

An unreadable expression comes over his face. Then rage breaks through, swollen and red, nostrils flared, hair standing up, the pointed ear-tips stiffening. His whole body is a deadly weapon aimed at her. His eyes signal to her his wish to take her apart completely, to leave nothing of her. 'Don't try to get out of it,' he says. 'Tonight, when they reach here, *you* will kill them all. And you, too, will join me in drinking their blood.'

'I don't share your pishacha tastes.'

'It's time to change that,' he says coldly, before disappearing with his long, loping gait into the forest.

4

Our Lady of the Shala Trees

Whenever Hidimbi felt troubled she went to Vichitra for advice. After the early morning exchange with her half-brother that is where she heads. Dawn has widened into the dazzling brightness of mid-morning, but in the grove of shala trees, where the yakshi lives, it is as if the curtains have not yet been opened. There is a balmy, dream-like air that feels like freedom—a lack of definition, maybe an absence of time.

No one knows how old Vichitra is. It is hard to imagine her as anything but what she has always been: slender-waisted and round-hipped, with an unlined skin and a full mouth, a pair of large, brown, intelligent eyes that hint at having seen everything and finding it all faintly ironic. When asked her age, she insists that she is five hundred years old, at least. She claims to know stories that no one else has heard. The strangest of them invariably begin with: 'It happened a long time ago, when I was a teeny-weeny seedling.'

Older than even Vichitra is the shala tree on which she lives. It has always been her home. It has endowed her with its spirit. The clean, stately lines of its trunk are reflected in her imperious nature; the coarse, robust grain lends an earthiness to her speech. Vichitra's shala tree is the oldest in the forest, the ancestress of all the shala trees. Women of the forest tribes call it the Mother Tree and leave their prayers and votive offerings at its base as their way of acknowledging that Vichitra, the lovely one, is ageless. A goddess. A guardian.

'You are so wise,' Hidimbi says, humbly. She knows that flattery works well with the yakshi. '*Please* tell me a way out. I cannot displease my elder brother as that would undermine him. He is, after all, a prince of the rakshasa tribe. But neither do I want to kill and eat an Arya or, for that matter, *any* human being. I tried human flesh once, because Hidimba insisted, but it disagreed with me. I was violently sick for days, couldn't stop throwing up.'

Vichitra listens with the neutral expression of someone who has just awakened from a sound sleep and is still adjusting to the change. She stifles a yawn. Then, as if collecting herself, she tries to look more animated. Clicking her tongue in sympathy, she says, '*I understand!*' This habit of stressing on words is unique to her; it makes her sound immeasurably wise.

The next instant, however, a roguish conspiratorial glint enters her almond-shaped eyes and she adds in an eager, gossipy tone, 'How Bakasura likes to boast about his exotic tastes! *Human* flesh is the food trend that he is trying to revive. He has such a cosy arrangement with the raja of Ekachakra who regularly delivers a live human at his doorstep.' She ticks off the items on her fingers. 'A few healthy cattle, a cartload of provisions and *one* citizen, preferably young to middle-aged as their flesh has the right proportion of fat and muscle.' She cackles. 'The king grandifies it by calling it a tribute. What would you call it?'

'Murder! Tyranny!' Hidimbi says hotly. 'The raja of Ekachakra is as cruel as Baka. He threatens his own people instead of protecting them. The sinner! Is his life so indispensable? Why can't *he* fight Baka?'

'Is that wise—to challenge someone much stronger than you? Isn't it simpler to appease him if that allows you to survive?'

'It allows *him* to survive…that coward raja!'

Vichitra lifts her strong, sun-browned shoulders in a shrug. 'In exchange for the tribute Ekachakra gives him, Baka *ensures* that the kingdom is protected from all threats, including other rakshasas. It may surprise you to know that the citizens have found the raja's solution—to sacrifice a few in order to save the many—to be practical. Feed the fiend and protect yourself, is the raja's motto. His people have readily adopted it. They have evolved a fair method: once a household sends a member to the forest, that family is considered to have discharged its duty and is left alone.'

Hidimbi is silent, her teeth chew the right edge of her lower lip. After a while, she says, 'The raja is only buying time. It's foolish of him. There are just two options for a rakshasa: either he dies in a fight or—and one must admit that this is rare—he lives a very long life. Instead of allowing the problem to continue, the raja must see it as a challenge and find a way to end it. Is there really no one who can kill Baka and put a stop to his tyranny?'

'Hmm. Another rakshasa maybe, but you know that they do not fight each other now that there are only a few left. These wars that the Aryas *love* to start will be the death of us all.'

'Then one has to find a rakshasa ready to pit himself against Baka. Trick him into it. Talk him into it. Make him believe that he, too, is threatened. He will surely fight. A true rakshasa never thinks of appeasement.'

'Ooh! We're *devious*, aren't we?' Vichitra chortles.

Hidimbi's seriousness crumbles and she grins back. But, recalling the reason she has come to see Vichitra, her face clouds again. 'Don't think that I'm afraid of facing an enemy. I can take on anyone who threatens the forest, but this killing of fugitives seems…unnecessary. There is a female with them too.'

Vichitra pats her shoulders. 'Stop *worrying* so much,' she says calmly. 'Lie down on that stone slab. You could do with a massage. We can talk at the same time.'

Vichitra's massages are an ordeal. Besides pinning down the victim, her technique involves squeezing, pressing, pulling, kneading. Hidimbi looks as if she is about to refuse but thinks the better of it and lies flat on her stomach. Digging her long, pointy fingers into Hidimbi's thick mass of curls, Vichitra says, 'Do you know what is the most *remarkable* thing about you?'

'My hair?'

'It's a *mess*.'

'My figure?'

'Certainly not! There's *no* shortage of shapely women in our world.' Vichitra elegantly tilts her head back as if to embody her words. 'Our curves will exalt us. Sculptors, artists, dancers will keep us alive *for ever*. Women will *pray* for hips as wide as ours.'

'Then?' prompts Hidimbi impatiently. 'What is so extraordinary about me?'

'It is *who* you are—a rakshasi.'

'I am. So what?'

'Pay attention to what I'm about to tell you,' says the yakshi, speaking slowly. Her fingers apply a stronger pressure, as if compelling Hidimbi to feel the weight of her message. 'The Aryas are obsessed with storytelling. When your story is told, no one will dream of asking the simple questions that have always been asked about young women everywhere: is she pretty? What is her skin like? Hair? Waistline? Smile? Shape and colour of her eyes?'

Hidimbi looks offended. 'Are you trying to say, in your own roundabout way, that I do not have a single feature that may be considered worthy of a compliment?'

'You are beautiful, my princess, but even so you will be seen only as a rakshasi.' Seeing Hidimbi's disbelief, Vichitra gives a long sigh. 'Let me explain…The Aryas are powerful. They consider themselves superior to everyone. They think that it's only normal that they make the rules for *everyone*. By their rules, forest dwellers are polluted races with mixed bloodlines and deviant ways.'

'*Deviant?* Different, yes but—'

'To them different *is* deviant. They make the rules, remember. Also, rakshasas, the most violent of the forest tribes, are destroyers of their religious sacrifices. Thus, in breed and creed, you are their opponent. Naturally, when they tell your story they will use opposites to describe you.'

'Opposites of what? What do you mean?'

'They believe that rakshasas are everything that they are not: ugly, unkempt, unpleasant, untamed, uncivilised, inhuman. Night-wanderers. Shape-shifters. Cattle-lifters. They revel in describing a rakshasa's general horribleness. Ginormous. Lewd and gluttonous. The rakshasa appetite, which *you* may think is merely healthy, *is* the subject of much prurient gossip among them.'

'They like to discuss what we *eat?*'

Vichitra nods vigorously. 'For them, all creatures are labelled by their dietary practices. We *are* what we eat.'

'In that case, I must be a combination of smoked pork and steamed wild mustard greens. It is what I ate yesterday, will eat today and probably tomorrow as well—it was a big wild boar that I killed.'

'See what I mean? The Aryas don't know hunger the way forest-dwellers do. They feel superior because they *grow* the food they eat, while the forest tribes live on whatever they can lay their hands on.'

Hidimbi nods mournfully. 'Sometimes even laying hands on food is difficult. Our food runs away from us. We are forever hungry.'

'Since they are assured of their food, it is that inordinate hunger that they regard as evil. Only someone who has never known real hunger will call a tiger a predator and a deer a prey. In their stories rakshasas eat human flesh. It makes them appear absolutely despicable. They don't understand that some rakshasas like to try out exotic meats. For instance, Bakasur and Hidimba. It's only a food fad, but it taints all rakshasas. Hence you, a rakshasi, will also be judged as totally vile.'

'*Vile?* But I ate a tiny morsel...just once,' wails Hidimbi in frustration. 'I didn't even like it. This is so unfair!'

'It is what it is.' Suddenly Vichitra giggles. 'Maybe there is some truth in it, too. I remember that your mother once bit off your father's ear.'

'I remember it too,' Hidimbi says with a severe, disapproving look. 'That was passion, she claimed. His ears stuck out, she said.'

'That's right, it was just an exploratory nibble. The gandharva *was* good-looking enough to eat and we all fancied him.' Vichitra gleefully watches as Hidimbi's face reddens. 'All the same, Hariti's bite was deep enough for the musician in him to discover the *highest* notes of his own vocal chords,' she says archly. 'His screeches tore through the forest. Soon after that he ran away—just as we'd all predicted. Not seen any sign of him and his veena since that day. Or of your mother. She went *chasing* after him. Maybe it was true love, after all. Who knows where they are now, making music together, one fervently hopes.'

Hidimbi sighs and turns around to lie on her back. Vichitra glances down at her and smiles. She applies gentle punches on her upper arms. After some time, Hidimbi shakes off her melancholy and resumes the conversation.

'Hidimba is half pishacha and pishachas don't see any difference between one kind of flesh and another. It's all food to them.'

'Maybe pishachas, as a race, have gone through hard times in the past—when there was nothing else to eat, not even bats, rats, cockroaches and worms. In such a situation, I suspect that even a rakshasa, too, would not be choosy.'

'What do you mean?'

'Only that for the Aryas, the anarya are less than human. Little people deserve fewer choices.'

'*Little* people! It seems like the ultimate degradation. We would not be little people if we could, like them, grow our own food, create new choices for ourselves. I remember that my mother was turning into a vegetarian. She used to say that it was simpler to pick the right berries and dig up edible tubers than catch and skin a porcupine.'

Vichitra grimaces. She looks down at her own

perfectly manicured pair of hands and says, 'I wouldn't recommend either.'

'You can afford not to. With their generous offerings, your worshippers ensure that you never go hungry.'

A quiet smug smile. 'I'm equally generous with my blessings.'

'Some of my aunts don't eat meat anymore,' Hidimbi says. 'I'm thinking of giving it up as well.'

'To *live* you have to kill something else that lives. Plants have a life too. And an afterlife—in which *they* devour those who killed them.' Vichitra pummels her shoulder with extra force. 'You aren't *getting* the point, are you?'

'Oww!' Hidimbi winces. 'What point?'

'People are *scared* of you if they believe that you eat raw flesh and drink fresh blood. A reputation for ferociousness is a *good* thing! The Aryas realise the value of it better than us.'

Hidimbi raises an eyebrow in query.

Vichitra explains. 'We are all descendants of the same Prajapati, all born of the wives of Rishi Kashyap, yet *they* give such fanciful, bellicose names to their boys. Beloved-of-the-gods, Steady-in-war, One-without-a-foe, Bold-and-splendid, Conqueror-of-enemies. Do you know why they do that?'

'No. Tell me.'

'Because they understand the language of power. They reserve naming for what matters most. Nothing is more important for a warrior than having sons. Sons are destroyers of enemies. A long, noble lineage is made up of heroic names. And what names do rakshasas have?' Vichitra begins to shake with mirth as she enumerates. 'Pot Ears, Three Heads, Headless Torso. As if they are all born losers!'

Hidimbi grins, then shakes her head. 'Well, rakshasas, if allowed to live, can live forever, but they rarely keep the looks they were born with. For example, Hidimba and Bakasur. Between them they have every deformity you can think of: cauliflower ears, broken jaws, dislocated shoulders, blinded eyes, smashed noses. Such are a rakshasa's pickings from a fight. The relics that they love to show off. It is proof that a rakshasa never backs away from a clash. I've had my share too. Once, when I was quite young, I lost a clump of hair in a fight with a bear.'

'And what did you give the bear?'

'A sore head for days,' Hidimbi replies with a laugh. 'He gives me a wide berth till today. Hmm. I wonder what the Aryas would think of our female names. For instance, would they consider Iron Mouth as the name of a loser?'

'More like the name of a dangerous woman.'

Hidimbi turns to look directly at her. 'And Long Sharp Nails?'

Vichitra's expression becomes grim. 'That was the name *they* gave her, Surpanakha. Her real name was Meenakshi.' Her voice fills with sorrow. 'And *she* was a princess of Lanka, the golden city, the pride of the rakshasas. Those were gold-tinted days for all of us. I was younger then. I remember how we all admired Meenakshi's style and tried to copy it, *including* the sharp, long nails. Of course, no one could match hers. *She* pampered her nails to perfection, painting them in fiery shades. Yes, she was bold, dangerous, mean and *absolutely irresistible.* She also had marvellous tattoos all over her skin, though a few prudish people, like her brother Vibhishan, found the artwork too racy for their taste… And there was that ruby-and-diamond nose-ring she sported. It immediately drew attention to her beautiful long nose!' She falls silent again for a few minutes, then says more briskly, 'In their accounts the Aryas also call her the root of woe. Both sides blamed *her* for the war that destroyed Lanka.' She tosses her head defiantly. 'So what? A woman who is badly wronged *should* do her best to bring woe to the wrong-doers! How else will they learn? What happened to poor Meenakshi was terrible but, well, it illustrates my point. The forest—and the beings that live in it—can protect themselves from all kinds of predators, but not from *them*. Burn, burn, burn! That's all they know.'

'But Lanka was burnt down by a vanara.'

'And *who* sent that vanara there?' demands Vichitra, indignantly. 'That's another thing they are good at—turning people from the same world *against* each other, even brother against brother.' Vichitra sends Hidimbi a sidelong glance and adds, 'Maybe sister against brother too.'

'*Oh!*' says Hidimbi resentfully. 'So, you too think that Hidimba is right and eating them is the answer.'

'A bit extreme, I agree,' says Vichitra. 'Just think of it as the pishachas do, another variety of red meat.' Seeing Hidimbi's disgusted look, she says with some exasperation, 'Do you even know how many shala trees have been cut down to build Arya homes? If they aren't stopped soon, neither you nor I will *have* a forest to call our own anymore.'

'But—'

'*You* are a rakshasi,' Vichitra says pointedly. 'You are born of *this* soil. You are also among the last of your tribe. If you want to protect this forest and save its people from extinction then you have to get over this squeamishness. You do not know their capacity for violence or treachery. And there's something else.'

'What?'

Vichitra eyes her thoughtfully for a few moments before replying. 'You've grown into a lovely young woman, but I hope you will be wise when the time comes to choose your mate. Rakshasis lose their hearts easily. They aren't choosy about it, that's their trouble… because losing it to an Arya only brings them grief. Take Meenakshi's example. I can never forget how she *looked* after her nose was sliced off.' She breaks off with a shudder, then says, 'Girl, *experience* is the best teacher. What has once been proven should not be tested a second time. The Aryas are dangerous because their beliefs are different. Their world is nothing like our jumbled-up ways. It is logical and well-defined. There is nothing random about it because its order is determined by reason: everyone is allotted a place and given an identity by which that person must live. Every man, every woman has to live within their boundaries.'

'I don't understand.'

Vichitra sends her a look of sadness and affection. 'You don't…how can you? This forest is all you know, its ferocity, but also its freedom—to live in the moment. Wild creatures do not worry about the future. Their lives begin and end without a discourse. They have no use for stories.'

'How is the Arya world different?'

'Simply put, it is the way they look at the world—as

segregated. Order against chaos, upper against lower, inner against outer, pure against impure, male against female, believers against non-believers. They also set strict limits on what is proper conduct and what is not, especially so for women. They like to marry women who are chaste, quiet, *pure bred. You* deviate too much from what is acceptable. To them everything about you is grotesque. Too big, too flashy, too loud, too many intersecting bloodlines. A relationship with your kind is not an option. If, however, you feel attracted to one of them…' she flounders for the right word and says gloomily, 'don't *expect* anything but the worst consequences for yourself.'

'Attracted? Me? Never!' Hidimbi looks outraged.

'Don't be so sure. Cunning is their weapon. Shedding blood is easy when you know that the toughest victories are won in the mind. They know how to win.'

'Then one must learn to deny them those victories.'

The yakshi is silent for a moment, then she slowly tilts her head to one side as if yielding to some unseen power. 'Good thinking, but it's not so easy in practice. Just remember what I said. *Don't* expect an encounter with them to end well for you.'

5

First Love

Twilight is Hidimbi's favourite time of the day. Her tree-sitting hour. From her sky house in the shala tree, the changing colours of the sunset look even more beautiful when deepened by the indigo of the approaching night. She is perched on a fork in the middle branches where the foliage is the most dense. In Hidimbi's childhood, the tree-house her mother built had been her playpen. Now, in the shala's rootedness and strength, she finds the reassuring sense of continuity that comes from a solid old friendship.

She loves the tree for the many memories of her mother that it keeps evergreen. Some of the memorabilia is the graffiti that Hariti had scratched on the bark. Hidimbi sees the series of intertwining hearts as the reminders of a life lived passionately; Hariti was never one to hold back in love. Occasionally, she finds a trinket—a bracelet carved out of bone, a necklace made of cowrie shells, a pair of coloured feather ear danglers—tucked away in a tree hollow and recognises these, too, as her mother's possessions.

There is something in the day's dying that always leaves her in a state of sweet melancholy. A wind rises within her, singing the refrain of loneliness mingled with a soft ache that even the constant companionship of the forest cannot quench. This ache is new, not easy for her to understand. Her father had created elegant tunes that she still half-remembers, but watching the green branches rising to kiss the sky's face, different, more primeval rhythms tremble inside her, as if her whole being is a harp waiting to be played.

Was this what her mother had meant when she spoke of love? She remembers, with sadness, one of her last conversations with Hariti.

❖

Maybe one day you will understand why I *have* to find your father again, Hariti had said. He loved me, but he was like the sun and the moon, an eternal traveller. Just passing through. I cannot wait an eternity for him to return. What if he never finds his way back to me? And what if he eventually does, but I would have lost my mind by then? I have to go looking for him now because he alone can set me free.

Aren't you free now? Hidimbi asked. Free of him.

No, Hariti replied. I was someone else *before* I ever set eyes on him. From that moment, I was different. I cannot explain it more clearly, but when I was with him something changed. Giving became more important than receiving.

Sure, it did. While you grubbed around for things to feed him, all he did was stare at the clouds and sing nostalgically of freedom, as if *he* was the caged bird.

He was. He came here to do penance for something he had done. A life of austerities was what he wanted. But I fell in love with him at first sight. Rakshasa magic has its uses. I charmed him and when the enchantment wore off, I used my powers to keep him in the forest.

But you also used the same magic to please him in every way you could. You were constantly renewing yourself for him. You changed yourself to look good in his eyes. Not just your hair but also your face looked different, your speech too seemed different—it became slow, as if you were sifting the words and picking only those that would appeal to him.

I know…I so wanted to keep him with me. It was in my power to fulfil some of his desires. I tried to give him everything he wanted but it wasn't good enough, because *I* was the one seeking…I wanted a kind of permanence that he could not give me.

Enslavement comes naturally when one loves?

I did not think of it as enslavement then...I thought that the meaning of life came down to our bodies alone. And for a while it did. But it didn't last. He wasn't content with me, he was just being patient, *suffering* me...Besides giving him a lot that he didn't ask for, *I* asked for too little. That was my mistake. Daughter, listen to me. What once was will never be again. I may love someone. I hope I will. But *not* in the same way. I am telling you this because I want you to understand something else: love you must. Serve the one you love, too, but never make him the centre of your world. Don't live merely for his smile. Don't make him a god. Don't give anyone the power to release you. Look for it within yourself. Or you will become what I am now, a shrivelled skin of my former self, only the bones left inside. He cut me off from myself. I must find a way to regrow. I must repossess myself. It is important to me.

❖

A light breeze riffling through the broad leaves runs its fingers through her hair and kisses her brow as if wanting to sweep away her confusing thoughts. Slow down, the shala tree says. Listen to your heartbeat and mine. They are keeping time together, isn't that beautiful?

Overhead, hordes of noisy parrots in green,

undulating waves—specked with the red of their beaks—fly home to their nests. From their conversation it is clear that they have raided the wild mango groves further south along the banks of the river. A tiny shower of yellow and black descends from the sky and with a slight flurry settles on her shoulder. It is a female golden oriole, a relatively new friend. A few summers ago, on an unbearably scorching day, the bird, dazed by the heat, had literally fallen out of the sky. Hidimbi had revived her. Now the oriole has a full nest of her own, but still drops by from time to time for a catch-up chat.

In short, lucid tweets she delivers the news: seven human beings have died in the fire near the town of Varnavat. A boat has crossed the river.

'A fisherman's boat?'

'A boat big enough for six people and the two boatmen.'

To Hidimbi, the idea of crossing a river by a boat is alien. One hops across streams and thundering waterfalls, swims across broad rivers. 'Where did it go?'

'Home.' The oriole gives her ear a sharp, impatient peck. 'And so must I...do you want to know the rest?'

'Yes, please,' says Hidimbi meekly.

'They are here, in *this* forest. They are unarmed.'

'Who are these people?'

'Runaways.'

'Is there a female among them?'

'Yes. Their mother, by the looks of her.'

'Do you know who all died in the fire?'

The oriole cocks her head to one side. 'King Pandu's five sons and their widowed mother. The seventh was the caretaker of the house. The news is all over the land. A new generation of the royal family wiped out, they are saying.'

'That *is* sad.'

'I thought you'd want to know…' The bird pauses meaningfully.

'Yes?'

'The fire spread to a palash forest outside Varnavat. *Our* young ones died too.'

'I know. I'm sorry. I really am!'

'*Wiped out!*'

'The young are always at risk, you know that. You have your own nest.'

'I do. I worry about them all the time. I wait for the day when they will fly away. It will be an empty nest, but in a good way…Be careful is all I'm saying. Something tells me that your life is about to change.'

Hidimbi sighs dispiritedly. 'Another warning. I've heard nothing else all day.'

'And now I must be on my way.' The oriole takes wing. With her departure, it is as if daytime magic too has fled. Night creeps in. Dark shadows marble the forest; nocturnal creatures, still asleep, mutter unquietly, their tongues forking out. The undead spirits begin to awaken and slowly stretch into life. Still, Hidimbi does not budge from her post.

❖

A huge, tousled head appears between the branches. Hidimba. She stares at him without blinking. It is a game from their childhood. He returns the deadpan look. Then he closes one eye in a slow wink.

The power to change form and shape, to grow as vast as the sky or as tiny as an ant, are modest examples of every rakshasa's supernatural powers, but Hidimba uses them as an attention grabber.

She sees that he has tied his talismans and donned the war paint. His face is covered in tiger stripes and his skin smeared in animal fat. Except for a stretch of tiger skin wrapped around his middle, his body is bare. The stench coming off him nauseates her almost as much as the sight of him.

He senses her revulsion. 'It's time,' he says in a hard voice. 'Go!' When she refuses to move, a mean look enters his face. 'You're a disgrace to the rakshasa name. I will see you banished from the forest.'

Cold menace ripples in him, reminding her of the crushing power of the monster snake that he had once fought and killed. The python's long skeleton now adorns his neck in loose circles, the bleached skull and open jaw jutting outward in a hideous reminder of its deadliness. Her mind goes grey. A passivity enters her. Though she hates herself for it, Hidimba has her in his grip. She is used to doing as told. Maybe, in meek compliance, too, there is a certain freedom. Her squeamishness, she reminds herself, is her own private affair. This is her fate—to be born a rakshasi. To live and die as one.

❖

The six intruders have found a safe spot under an ancient nyagrodha tree. The thick canopy allows them abbreviated glimpses of the star-studded sky. It may have been the sight of those distant stars, their steady twinkling so reassuring to travellers everywhere, that has encouraged them to fall into a deep sleep. Or it may be plain fatigue.

She studies them carefully, seeking from the arrangement of the supine bodies some tiny disclosure about their identities. Their sleeping faces are as inscrutable as death. The woman lies in the centre of the row. She has turned to one side. With her back curved, knees slightly curled towards her chest, and one arm cushioning her head, she looks as if she is guarding herself even in slumber. The four men, two on either side, are younger than her. They sleep on their backs, like warriors. They sleep not as if they are homeless, but as if they are secure in the rich life of their dreams. As if someone is watching over them. There should be a fifth man—where is he?

After a while, she hears a rustle in the bushes behind her. A family of warthogs emerges through the undergrowth. They come from the direction of a large pool. Their unusually brisk pace suggests that something or someone has alarmed them while they were quenching their thirst. A few minutes later, she hears a man's voice. Judging from the frequency and fluency of his curses, he is blundering through the darkness, as if the night itself is a long blind alley. She melts into the shadows. When he is very close to her, the man comes to a sudden stop. She freezes. Has he sensed her presence?

Her irises widen. An ancient instinct and training merge in her body, a savagery transforms her. She crouches slightly, preparing to attack. In that split second, before she springs at him, the man rushes forward, past her. She is aware of a blurred movement and the hollow sound of something dropping. A few splashes of water from the gourd pot he has been carrying fall on her. She waits for a while and hearing only silence, steps out of hiding and goes stealthily to the nyagrodha tree.

❖

Dead? All five dead?

That is his first thought for a heart-stopping moment. The forest is said to be enchanted and filled with evil spirits. *I should never have left them, not for a moment.* But who else was there to fetch water for their mother when she, poor woman, complained of a terrible thirst? His brothers had all looked at him expectantly. He is the strongest among them. He is tireless. They rely on his strength. *Did I linger too long at the lake? Were they attacked? By one or many? But there are no signs of a struggle.*

It occurs to him, at last, that they could be merely asleep. He steals up to each one of them and assures himself that everyone is breathing normally, steps back and looks for a spot from where he can keep an eye on his family. His muscles are knotted from the strain of the flight from the burning house. As they had made their way through the forest one by one, the others had flagged. Lifting them, bearing their combined weight, driven by a fear he couldn't fathom, he had continued to flee...He would never forget that running away. Bheem...running away like a coward? With a low moan he sinks to the ground. His body aches but it is a deeper agony that convulses him. Alone at last, he succumbs to the despair. Hunched, rocking himself, he allows the long pent-up emotions to surface and sheds tears.

❖

How peaceful they look. As if they trust me to let them sleep on. A child's faith. They don't know how tired I am. I, too, crave rest. But I must keep awake. Though we had planned the escape for months, it was still very tough. We had to get as far away as quickly as we could from the Kuru lands, before dawn. The river was our immediate destination, but, at night, with only the stars to guide us through the forest, it seemed twice as far. The boat and the boatmen were waiting, as arranged. Uncle Vidur, at least, did not let us down. He has been our sole friend all these years…The wind, too, was favourable last night and, despite the strong current, we crossed the river quickly.

On the other bank loomed the dark, threatening mass of trees. Another forest, one that we did not know how to navigate. Yet, we were pushed to run. Our doubts chased us: had our plan succeeded? Had that obnoxious Purochan burnt to death? It would be disastrous if he had somehow managed to survive. The tribal woman and her family were unconscious from the smoke when I last saw them. They are surely dead, but will their remains convince everyone that *we* have died?

We are dead.

Maybe that is why I want nothing more than to lie down, to understand what it is to be lifeless, to curl up into the earth's warmth and feel nothing. But I *have* to stay awake, at least till one of my brothers wakes up and takes over the watch. We must be on our guard all the time from now on. No one must know that the Pandavas are alive.

Poor, tired souls...they sleep on the bare ground. It makes no sense. My mother, who has known every comfort, slept on the softest of beds fanned by servants, lies down like a destitute woman. A queen, my mother, sister of Vasudev, daughter of Kuntiraj, daughter-in-law of the great Kurus, wife of Pandu, mother of us five—look at her pitiable state now!

Royalty should sleep in utmost comfort, but here is my elder brother, Yudhisthir, who was born to rule a kingdom. Here lies Arjun, the world's finest archer, who, like our father Pandu, was born to conquer. And there are the twins, golden-eyed, handsomer than the gods, who look up to us, their older brothers. Tonight, they all sleep like the dispossessed.

How did we end up like this—homeless? Who is responsible for our present condition? Who else but our own kin...Lucky is the man who has no jealous relatives: like a solitary tree in a village, he is valued for what he contributes. Such a man is respected for himself. Fortunate, too, is the man who has brave and worthy dharma-following relatives, for he is strengthened by his connections. In such families, everyone prospers, everyone lives in harmony. Like the trees in a natural forest, they help each other to grow and thrive. But evil-minded Dhritarashtra—who only pretends to follow dharma—and his sons have *always* seen us as the interlopers. They want nothing else but to drive us out of our father's kingdom. *They want us dead.* If our being alive is a threat to Duryodhan, he will not rest as long as he knows we are still living...where will this pursuit of us end? I will keep a watch over my family for now, but how can I prevent the dangers dawn will bring? *Damn you, Duryodhan!* Enjoy your own slumber tonight. Though you don't deserve it, Yudhisthir still thinks of you as a brother. He has ordered me to leave you alone. I cannot disobey. Otherwise, by now, I would have single-handedly destroyed all of you for this treachery.

❖

Watching him, Hidimbi is mystified by his posture. Has he too fallen asleep? She is reluctant to attack him and wonders if she should prod him awake first. After a few moments of indecision, she steps out into the open and with soft footfalls approaches him. As if sensing her presence, the man lifts his head. The dull, concussed look in his eyes is not that of someone returning from the margins of sleep. He is a man battered by anguish. Her heart contracts as she instinctively feels his pain, then hurries towards him, like a tune finding its song.

Love, like poetry, starts in the middle. Who can say on which day, at what time and where, the first seed is dropped in the ground just when it is ready to receive it? At the precise moment that he is cursing Fate, it appears before him—dressed up as a beautiful young woman. He closes his eyes briefly to clear the fog in his brain, but the shadowy vision does not dissolve. Instead, it grows more real as if it aims to conquer the depth of his despair by its sheer vitality. He notes, with a sense of surprise, how tall she is, nearly the same height as him. But her face has the ineffable beauty of someone much younger in years. Her eyebrows arch like a bird's wings; the deep brown eyes are grave, concerned; the cheekbones high, the lips full with the promise of pleasure. The real allure, however, lies in her body, in its voluptuous curves. Her legs are long, lean, bare and graceful—a dancer's legs. There is in her the strange evanescent quality of a mirage, as if she might, in the very next instant, change form, merge into the forest, become a feral creature wrought from a different forge.

Around them the darkness dissipates. It is suddenly full of whimsy. Only her gaze, now cool and wary, a mirror image of his own, seems real. In that moment blooms an immediate recognition: there had been only one before, now there are two. The same wind, the same roar, signifying an immense zest for living. Between them, they get the sense that a future can birth itself. It is in their blood: the poison and its antidote. As if aware of it, that they are now in a different territory, a separate forest which has them in a tangle, both speak together, the same words, too: who are you?

Neither replies.

Hidden in the undergrowth and in the thick curtains of foliage, sharp-eyed nocturnal creatures watch them with the bored disdain that comes from having witnessed too many such dalliances. A canny owl, watching the encounter, grumbles to himself. It is the same old script. The manly hero in despair; enter the heroine, delicately. And neither could be bothered to remember the lines. The owl hoots in disgust. Once. Twice.

Hidimbi looks up and shakes her fist at the bird. The owl sends her a huffy look, fluffs its feathers and flies off. A string of curses from Hidimbi gives it chase.

'Now, don't tell me that you understand the language of the birds,' Bheem's tone is mocking.

She looks at him without replying. 'I do,' she says, eventually.

He raises an eyebrow. 'What did the bird say?'

She replies truthfully. 'No good will come of this.'

He sends her a startled look and, after a brief pause, asks, 'Who was that prophecy meant for—you or me?'

She likes the sound of his voice, its deep rasp. 'For us,' she says.

'*Us?*' He sends her a quizzical look.

'Oh! Don't pay attention. The silly bird says it all the time. It's the kind of *wise* prophecy about which you can never be completely wrong.'

He says nothing. There is something so superior, dismissive and half-joking in her tone that he has a feeling that she really does understand the languages of birds.

She tilts her head to one side and looks frankly at him. A fighter: his shoulders are strong, the muscles of his arms are well-developed. A wrestler perhaps. Maybe even a mace warrior. There are tell-tale signs of a violent man about him. A haughty, taunting air. Surprisingly, the general topography of his face is undamaged. While that is a refreshing change, she wonders how he has managed to keep all his features intact. Not even a scar to mar the evenness and symmetry of his outline. Has he never been challenged to a fight? Does he, like some animal species, have the ability to grow back a damaged limb? His skin is golden-hued, hair thick and long. There is an earthy magnetism about him but also splendour and gravitas. A new thought occurs to her: maybe he is a god. Only an immortal god would have that kind of self-assurance. Yes, he must be a god, a knower of eternity. Suddenly Forever itself is a possibility, a new world waiting in the wings.

With elaborate casualness, a feigned air of boredom, she says, 'Now that we've been properly introduced, tell me your name.'

After the briefest of pauses, he replies. 'Vrikodar.'

Wolf waist. Lean and mean. A name she understands. 'Doesn't sound pompous, at all,' she says, approvingly.

He frowns. 'What do you mean?'

'Nothing.' After a moment she adds, 'It suits you. I had a wolf pup once. He was always ravenous. Are you like that too—perpetually hungry?'

As if in reply, his stomach makes a gurgling sound. Famished, it says.

She smiles knowingly.

He wonders if she is about to produce a feast out of nowhere? Is she a yatudhani, a sorceress? Worse, she may be a dakini, a flesh eating demoness. That would explain her presence in this lonely spot at this hour. Only those with evil in their heart wander about at this time of the night.

There is a rustle in the branches above. The owl has returned, this time with a message for her from her brother. Short, direct and finite. *Kill him!*

'This forest is under the spell of a powerful rakshasa,' she says, a bit nervously. 'It is not safe for you to be here, not even for a moment. You must leave. I can help you, but you will have to come with me. *Now.*'

Her words make him tense. He and his family have been on the run for a night and day. They have run as fast and as far as they could manage, but it appears as if it is not enough. Wherever they go, monsters lurk. A rakshasa named Duryodhan wants them dead and now this new danger. Something in him rebels. He nods his head in the direction of the sleepers and says curtly, 'I cannot wake them. They are tired.'

'Not them. Just you.'

'You want me to leave them behind?'

'Why not? All of you don't stand a chance against the mighty Hidimba. He is twice your size and relishes the taste of raw human flesh. If you take my help, at least *you* won't end up as his food and drink. He likes human blood even better. Sweeter than mother's milk, he describes it.'

He sends her a look of loathing. 'Go away! I don't want your help.'

'Don't be reckless.'

'*Leave!*'

The sudden anger in his voice makes her clench her fists. Her heart begins to hammer painfully, but she stays her ground.

He stares at her suspiciously. 'How do I know that

this is your real form? You could be from a family of yatudhanas. Maybe the offer to help me is just a lure and *you* intend to eat me. Are you playing with me? I am warning you: don't.'

'Trust me. I am your well-wisher. I think that you are more valuable alive than dead.' Seeing that he is not convinced, she sighs. 'Listen. You are not to my taste. I am not in the least tempted to eat you. Nor do I want you to become someone else's feast. Therefore, *you* must be the one to leave. Don't waste time arguing about it. Take my offer. It is genuine. If you insist, I will carry not just you, but your entire clan to safety.'

'*Carry?*' A note of amused interest enters his voice. 'You carry us? All of us?'

'I can—if I have to.'

'Where to? Where will you keep us safe?'

'Inside a cloud or an underwater cave. I could hide you deep at the bottom of a giant lotus that grows in the sea, or in a fortress guarded by a ring of fire and an army of pishachas. There are several good hiding places I know of.'

He sends her a dark look. 'It's clear you *are* one of them. A dakini, a yatudhani, an apsara or a yakshi. Don't bother to deny it.'

'Why should I?' Like a wild creature baring its incisors as a warning, she adds, 'I'm proud of who I am.'

'Oh! And who are you?'

'A rakshasi.'

'I thought so! You were pretending all this while to be someone else, but I wasn't fooled. So, you are a rakshasi and you naturally fancy *me* as your next meal.'

'No...not as a meal.' She gives him a long, explicit look.

He becomes very still. She wonders why he is uncomfortable. What is amiss with her words? She has merely hinted at her interest in him and solicited his. She waits for him to say something. Her heart is suddenly galloping.

'What is your name?' he asks, at last.

'Hidimbi.'

'Hidimbi? But you just said that Hidimba is—

'The king of the rakshasas. He is my half-brother, too. A dangerous sort he is. Intends to crush your bones and drink your blood.'

'Hah! Right! You said that before.' There is an annoyed snap to his voice. 'How do I make you understand? I *cannot* run away leaving my mother, my elder brother and my younger siblings to become food for a rakshasa.'

'Mother, elder brother, younger brothers.' She counts off on her fingers. 'Thrice pledged, are you?'

'What?' He sends her a wild look. 'Yes! *Three* reasons

for turning down your offer, but they add up to the same thing. I have to protect my family.'

Secretly, she is impressed. 'Wake them up then,' she says, casually.

'No! Let them sleep. You have no idea what they have been through. And don't worry about me. There is no rakshasa, gandharva, yaksha or daitya who can hold out against me.'

'Oh! Really? How does a mere man—'

'I am not a mere man!'

'In this forest you are. How do you—'

'No more questions from you,' he says, bringing his palms together in a mock appeal. 'And no more suggestions, either. As for the rest, do as you please. Stay around if you want to. Or, *go*...go and send your revolting rakshasa brother to me. I'll take him on. I'm not afraid of anyone.'

Barely are the words out of his mouth when a mighty wild wind begins to rage through the forest. The trees shake violently. Their branches creak and snap, crashing to the ground, as if blighted by lightning. The forest floor sizzles and cracks open in places, revealing thin glimpses of fiery caverns. A reddish, foul-smelling fug thickens the air. It is as if the entire world is reassembling itself on a new plane—a battlefield. Then an immense, evil darkness appears. Hidimba stands before them.

Massive he is. His face grim. Inflamed by rage, his eyes trained on his sister are giant candle flames, yellow-red, piercing. They gleam even more ominously as they take in the look on her face; its soft radiance is that of a full moon. He sees, too, how she has beautified herself in a gauzy garment of spider thread and butterfly wings, dressed her hair with wildflowers and her body adorned with ornaments made of mother-of-pearl. There is, also, the fragrance she gives off, wanton as the elusive airs of spring. A scent contrived to create ardent longing. An open invitation to all healthy males; the scent drives him to a white-hot fury, directed solely at her.

'You shameless woman!' He spits out the words. 'Was this why I sent you here? To tempt our enemy to be your lover? Stupid woman, that will *never* be. You tarnish our name. You dishonour our ancestors. I feel like killing *you.* I will deal with him and the other lot later.' He rushes at her, arms raised to grip her neck.

He is much stronger than her, but she too knows how to fight. However, before she can change her stance in readiness, there is an interruption.

'Hurt a woman, will you?' The voice is contemptuous but also challenging. Its owner bars Hidimba's way. 'Take me on first.'

'Get out of my path,' growls the rakshasa. 'This has nothing do with you.'

'You cannot harm her. I will not allow it.'

'*What?* How dare you! She is *my* sister. I sent—'

'Yes! *You* sent her to me. *You* planned this.' Bheem says. 'Don't blame her. She tried her best, but I'm a tough nut to crack, even for a rakshasi who knows how to turn on the charm. The trouble is that I am irresistible to women and she has already confessed her desire for me. She wants to be my protectress. But I'm astounded at your cowardice. Instead of looking after your sister, you send her to kill us so that you can eat us. You should have come yourself...why didn't you do that? Were you scared? Despite your size, you are a faint-hearted fellow. Brag and boast, that's all you know.'

Fury makes Hidimba splutter. 'I will—*kill*—'

'Shh...' Bheem gestures to him to be quiet. 'Don't flash your eyes and roar at me like an empty thundercloud.' He points toward the nyagrodha tree. 'Can't you see they are all sleeping peacefully? Let us continue our discussion a bit further away. There is a clearing nearby and we will disturb no one while I give you a few useful lessons—in courtesy towards women *and* in hand-to-hand combat.'

'Don't try to impress my foolish sister by provoking me to fight you,' Hidimba says. 'I'll see to her later. First, it's your turn. Right here, right now.'

'They say that the life in the forest is nasty, short and brutish.'

'It is—for some. Say your prayers.'

Bheem laughs. 'What I meant was that *you* have obviously lived too long. Killing is all you know. Do you keep a count of how many you have killed? Eating human flesh and drinking human blood are your pleasures, I've been informed. Your sister will see how I am going to wipe the ground with you. After I'm done, it will be the hyenas, jackals and vultures who will lick your blood and tear at your flesh, while all the men and women who live in this forest will thank me for ridding them of your evil presence.'

Despite himself, Hidimba is impressed by his opponent's bravado. He sniffs the air to catch the man's scent. Animal meat, sweat, mud, water, smoke. But he also gets a rare smell—of power, fearlessness. It annoys him even as it warns him that this battle is not going to be an easy one. 'Stop showing off and start fighting. Come on!'

'No, *you* come on.' Bheem throws his mighty arms wide open.

The rakshasa raises his hands, as if they are clubs, and charges. With a crowing laugh, Bheem seizes his lower arm, twists him around so that he is off-balance and flings him aside. Hidimba crashes into the base of a tree and sends the different wild creatures that inhabit it into orbit. When he has righted himself, Hidimba flings his body again at Bheem.

The impact feels like an earthquake. Bheem has miscalculated the rakshasa's strength. Though his face maintains a hint of a sneer, his mind sends a message to his limbs: *stop mucking about. Focus and hit him, or he will be dangerous.*

He grabs the rakshasa's neck and smells his hot foetid breath as they grapple. The fangs are dangerously close. He looks into the amber eyes and sees the unrelenting, senseless fury in them. He pushes the dark, hairy face as far back as he can, simultaneously squeezing the jaw. There is a crunching noise as the rakshasa's jawbones shatter. Blood squirts in a red stream into the air. A few shaky teeth, among them two of the fangs, fall out. Hidimba cups them in his palm and looks at them as if he cannot understand what they are doing there. His mouth fills up with the iron taste of his own blood. He spits it out.

Insults and abuses are a part of Bheem's strategy. As a mace warrior he knows the value of unnerving his enemy by hitting at an opponent's weakest spot: his pride. He jeers, 'Getting a taste of your own medicine, huh? How do you like it?'

In reply, the rakshasa roars so loudly that the Pandavas and their mother shoot out of the depths of their slumber. The brothers scramble to their feet and look around in confusion. At first, they can make out nothing except the haze, a maelstrom of wind, dust and uprooted trees. Then they see the two demons, indistinguishable from each other, battling like two rutting elephants. First one drags the other to his side, then the other does the same. One falls and the other stumbles and drops on top of him. Who is who? Is that Bheem?

Seeing the rakshasa pin Bheem down, Arjun shouts, 'Need any help, Brother? If you are tired, I can finish him off while Nakul and Sahadev guard our mother.'

'I can take care of him,' Bheem roars back.

'If you say so' Arjun says, sceptically. To him, the opponents seem to be equally matched in strength. 'Don't take too long to wipe him out. We must leave before dawn. Kill him before he uses his magic to trick you…If you aren't up to it, I can do it for you.'

At this, a tornado rises within Bheem and he attacks the rakshasa with renewed vigour. Lifting him above his head and spinning him around a few times, he taunts him. 'Good-for-nothing fellow! You *are* good for nothing except eating stale foul-smelling meat. Old and debased! Useless today, tomorrow and forever. You deserve to die a useless death. In the netherworld to which I will now send you, you *will* be useless forever.'

'Hey, Bheem,' Arjun goads, 'Save your breath. Finish him off quickly, or let me do it—if it's too much for you.'

'Stay out of it,' Bheem yells back. 'I am a kshatriya. Nothing is too much for my strength.' With a final burst of energy, he flings the rakshasa on the floor and kills him as he would an animal. A blood-curdling sound—beginning as the boom of a wet drum and turning into a bestial, wavering howl—leaves the rakshasa. The eerie cry floats over the forest. When it fades, there is pin-drop silence. Bheem holds the rakshasa's bloody trunk and places it on his knee. With one precise move, he folds it in two. As the sound of the ribs cracking reaches them, his brothers applaud. Bheem casts the body carelessly to one side.

'Congratulations!' Nakul says. 'Your first rakshasa kill.'

'But not the last,' adds Sahadev, grinning.

'Not a bad effort,' Arjun remarks with a mischievous look. 'Though you took too long to finish him. All those unnecessary feints.' Seeing Bheem bristle, he adds smoothly, 'Of course, you will argue that feints are a part of a good mace warrior's technique, their purpose being to tire and distract the opponent.'

'Criticise my technique all you want,' Bheem says brusquely. 'The fact is that it worked. Do you know *why* I was a better fighter? Because I was desperate to save my family…what I'd like to know is why were you so keen to butt in?'

'*Butt in*? No, no…I was only reminding you to speed things up. They say that rakshasa powers are strongest at twilight. Dawn, as you can see, is here. We cannot delay now. There is a town not far from this forest. We must head for it. By now, Duryodhan's men will be looking for us everywhere.'

'Duryodhan,' Bheem says curtly and spits on the ground. He sends the fallen rakshasa a long, thoughtful look. There had been a moment in the fight when powered by many years of simmering, his ever-present resentment had turned into rage. White-hot. All sense of the real was swept aside. In that moment, he had not known whom he was pulverising—Hidimba or Duryodhan. The two, in his imagination equal in their bestiality, had fused into one. And he, too, had felt a strange kind of unity with that hybrid creature, as if suddenly freed from the restraints that circumscribed his true nature. In its own way, the moment had felt sublime. He wipes his face with the back of his hand and scowls. 'I will kill Duryodhan, too, one day, but *his* will be a more terrible death, I promise you. He deserves that much.'

❖

Hidimbi kneels by her brother and stares in disbelief at his body. Its stillness makes no sense to her. This broken, twisted, unpicked-at-the-seams carcass that continues to speak in its combative style. His fists are clenched tight, as if preparing to inflict the next blow. His face is contorted in rage. Blood wells from his mouth. This is who I am, he seems to be saying. But like a king stripped of his crown, the malevolent power, the immorality that characterised him has somehow gone. In its place there is a strange gentility, a sense of calmness and poise, as if this end, somehow, befits his idea of himself: the death is a fair one. Not a human and not, despite his extraordinary powers, a god, he had lived on the cusp of both, yet independently, lawlessly. This end is not just fated but the best a monster like him can hope for. Unravelled, cut down to size, he is now just a corpse that, like any other, will be cleaned and washed by his kin before being left, as per the ancient funeral rites, for the vultures to feed on. Prayers will be said for the safe journey of his soul. And slowly the flesh will disintegrate and the bones picked clean.

Looking down at him, a deep sadness rises in her as she senses the loneliness of a half-breed, the ill-proportioned, the half-alive who must live forever on the borders of what is possible but also impossible. Was that the burden that had prompted her half-brother's peculiar self-loathing? Death has broken a gap in the invisible shield around him. It has brought home to her, her own loneliness too. Blood is blood, no matter where it comes from. The sap of life runs in everyone. The same stream. No one will call him a hero, no one will miss him terribly—yet his going matters to her. It matters even more because there was something heroic about the last fight he fought. His best fight. She was a witness.

The first rays of light swim in through the canopy. Rakshasas have always avoided this rose gold light, rakshogna; it is when their magical powers come crashing down. This dawn, she realises, is different from those past. Hidimba is gone, his power over her has gone with him. She can mourn her half-brother now by keeping only the good memories to herself. She reaches forward to close his eyes. But at that very instant they fly open again. The fading light in them focusses into sharp glowing pins that rise out of their sockets into the air and merge into a green point. For a moment the vaporous light hovers over his head uncertainly, then, as if pulled away by a magnetic force, it slides away and dissipates. His monstrous nose quivers one final time. As the last breath leaves it, he says in a voice that is just above a whisper, but filled with both relief and wonder, as if death is a luxury he can finally afford, 'Strange! There are no smells here.'

She observes that the intruders are leaving. Vrikodar, too, is among them. Where is *he* going?

'Wait!' she calls out. 'You cannot leave.'

They turn around and notice her for the first time.

She senses, in a glance, that something has changed: Vrikodar, in whom she had sensed a kindred spirit, has become someone else. A barrier, invisible but solid and immovable, has sprung up around him. He is not as different as she had thought. He is one with the rest. One of them.

6

The Proposal

Her garment, gauzy and flowing, as if it is made of mist, ripples in the light breeze. Behind her, the forest is still in semi-darkness. But she, with early sunshine streaming through her dress, appears fresh and dazzling. The men watching her wonder if she is a yakshini or a goddess.

Then she moves and they realise that she is not an otherworldly vision but a flesh and blood woman. Young, nubile, scantily clad. They cannot help but gape, their eyes loitering over her curves. All except for Bheem, who scowls and mutters something rude beneath his breath. However, a quick warning glance from Yudhisthir silences him.

Nothing escapes their mother's attention. Noticing her sons' keen interest in the young woman, Kunti sends them a sharp look that shuts, as if by magic, their half-open jaws and erases all expression of interest from their faces. Narrowing her eyes imperceptibly, she scans the young woman from head to toe. Her lips stretch in a tight, brief smile, as if this meeting is entirely normal. Somewhat imperious but entirely at ease, she greets the woman pleasantly enough. 'How lovely you look, Child, but aren't you a bit cold in those clothes? Here, take my wrap.' She removes the rough woven upper cloth she is wearing over her clothes and holds it out.

Hidimbi is startled by the gesture. 'I don't need it.'

'No, keep it on,' Kunti insists, her manner motherly but firm as she moves towards Hidimbi and drapes the shawl over her shoulders. Standing back, she says with a sympathetic smile, 'It is unusual to see a woman as young as you in a place like this. Are you alone?'

'Yes.'

'What is your name? Who are your people? Where is your home?'

'My name is Hidimbi. This forest is my home. I am...'

'The rakshasa's sister!' Bheem interrupts, scornfully. 'He sent her to kill us. Together they were planning to make a feast of us.'

His brothers look startled. They study the young woman with more guardedness, as if expecting her, any moment, to revert to a grotesque form complete with matted brown hair, bulging eyes, claws, bloated stomach and a long, blood-red tongue. Hidimbi returns their gaze calmly, without embarrassment.

Looking them over—so sleek, well-nourished and self-assured—she wonders if they are all devas in disguise. Are they really brothers? They look close in age, but do not share the same build or even the same facial features, except for the two youngest whose good looks are very similar. Yet, she senses an indescribable familiarity among all five, a rapport of blood and fate. They are a pack.

Ignoring them, she turns her attention to the woman, their mother, and addresses her. 'What he says is true. My brother sent me to kill you, but *I* decided not to.'

'How considerate of you,' says Kunti, adding with mild interest, 'But what made you change your mind?'

'Manmatha's arrow,' Hidimbi says. 'Desire pierced me—right here.' She places a hand on her bosom.

For a moment, Kunti looks blank. Then, as understanding floods in, a glint of amusement enters her eyes. She glances at Bheem who looks away sheepishly. 'Are you talking about your feelings for...*him*?'

'Yes. He knows what I mean. He feels the same way, too. Ask him! When Hidimba wanted to wring my neck, Vrikodar sprang to my defence. *He* challenged my half-brother to a fight. Why would he do that if he wasn't smitten too? Only a love-struck man would face up to a rakshasa *and* kill him. Only true love has that kind of strength. Although, I must say that Vrikodar turned out to be a surprisingly good fighter. No other man could have acted with the courage and skill he showed.'

Bheem's face turns purple-red. His brothers, listening intently, send him sly grins. All except Yudhisthir who responds to Hidimbi with his typical air of seriousness. 'You said that your brother was about to harm you when Vrikodar intervened. You may not know it, but in our tradition, for a man to raise a hand against a woman is considered low behaviour, not to be tolerated.'

'Is that so? Do your females not know how to defend themselves?'

'Let's just say that it is a man's duty to protect a woman, *any* woman, from being ill-treated.'

Unconsciously adopting his grave manner, Hidimbi says, 'If we are to talk of traditions, then it is my duty to tell you that we follow a very different one in the forest. A rakshasa will fight over a female only if he wants her as his mate. And then he will go all out to wrest her away from her relatives. Winning is important because it is a declaration of his interest in her. Vrikodar has won. He has won me in a fair fight. Of course, it helps if the female concerned is willing—*and I am!*'

Yudhisthir is dumbfounded. After a moment, he

says stiffly, 'These differences in our traditions are, no doubt, fascinating, but *we* cannot interpret this situation in the light of your custom. Bheem wasn't aware of your tradition, he merely did what *his* demanded of him.'

Hidimbi is crestfallen. 'Are you saying that he didn't do it out of a desire for me?'

Bheem makes a strangled sound.

Yudhisthir shrugs. 'Erm…something like that, yes.'

'Then *he* misread the situation,' Hidimbi says, coldly. 'It maybe your custom that females are not taught to defend themselves and expect their males to do it. Rakshasis are not as frail as your women. *I* neither sought Vrikodar's protection, nor did I expect it. Why then did he jump into a quarrel that had nothing to do with him? Yes, it would have been a tough fight against Hidimba, but I would not have folded under his assault. I know how to take care of myself. I offered, in fact, to protect you all from my brother. If Vrikodar had taken up my offer, none of this need have happened.'

Bheem is livid. 'It is an insult to me to suggest that I, a kshatriya, would need anyone's help to defend my family. Your brother was a rakshasa, the scum of this earth, *therefore* his death was fated at my hands. By killing him I have ended his evil reign. As for defending *you*, Rakshasi, no, I wasn't doing that either when I took your brother on. Nor was it my intention to kill him in order to marry you. I have no such desire.' Turning to his brothers, he says curtly, 'Let us not waste any more time in this godforsaken forest. It may be infested with more rakshasas.'

Hidimbi turns on him with sudden fury. 'This forest is not *infested* with rakshasas! It is our home. *You* are the infestation.'

A stunned silence greets this outburst.

Forcing herself to be calm, Hidimbi addresses Kunti and Yudhisthir. 'My brother was, like me, a guardian of the forest. Now that he is gone, the future of our tribe depends on me. I have to choose a mate. According to our tradition—which is as worthy as yours—Vrikodar has proven that he is a fitting partner for me. With his fighting skills, he will be an asset to our tribe. I like Vrikodar's deep sense of loyalty to you. I see an affinity between him and me. He, too, is a protector. As you are his first family, I am ready to make you mine too. I invite you all to make your home here. You need run no further.'

'We appreciate your hospitality,' Yudhisthir says. 'What makes you imagine that we are on the run?'

She studies him. Among the five, he is clearly the oldest. Though his appearance is less remarkable, he has an air of quiet authority. He speaks like he knows a lot and expects total attention from his audience. He looks like he appreciates honesty and has shown in his attitude a degree of willingness to listen to her.

'Not think…*I know*,' she says. 'The news is all over the land. There was a fire two nights ago. A widowed queen and her five sons from a powerful kingdom in Aryavarta were burnt to death. Maybe it was a sheer coincidence—maybe it was not—that a female and five males were seen running *away* from the general direction of the fire.'

'Seen by whom?'

'Creatures of the forest have reliable ways of communicating.'

Arjun begins to shake his head slowly from side to side in disbelief. Bheem glances at him. 'She knows the languages of birds,' he says. 'Her brother was a magician. Who knows what dark arts she too practices?'

Yudhisthir gestures to him to be quiet. 'Go on,' he says to Hidimbi.

'Who were the people who died? Who are you six? You are desperate enough to venture into rakshasa territory. It's true that males of your type do come to the forest, to hunt or to perform a fire ritual, but a *female*—never! I don't know who you are, but something tells me you are connected to that burning.'

'What do you mean?' Yudhisthir's voice is even. This creature is more intelligent than one would take her for, he notes mentally.

Hidimbi does not reply. To Kunti, she says bluntly, 'Your sons look like devatas, but *you* have the air of a ruler. Are you one?'

Bheem glares at her. 'Don't speak to my mother in that tone.'

'So! You *are* a queen,' says Hidimbi. 'A queen of Aryavarta.'

Kunti sends her an unreadable look, neither accepting nor rejecting the guess.

'Don't believe a word,' Bheem says to the others. 'She is a rakshasi. They all have long memories and are known to be vengeful. Violence is the only language they understand. I have a good mind to send her to the same place as her brother.'

'You will do nothing of the sort,' Yudhisthir says firmly. 'You have already killed a powerful rakshasa to protect us. Even if this sister of his harbours thoughts of revenge, what harm can a mere female do? You also need to remember that one's personal safety cannot be more important than one's dharma.'

Visibly forcing himself to be patient, Bheem says, 'I repeat, she is no *mere female* but a rakshasi—to the core. Don't trust her for a moment.'

'Why do you talk about me as if I am not here?' Hidimbi asks him indignantly. 'What have I done that you feel you cannot believe me? Did I lie to you? If

I were indeed your enemy, wouldn't I have joined Hidimba in fighting you? We rakshasas are not afraid of death…Believe me, your victory would not have been as simple then.' Turning to the others, she says half-entreating, 'Am I really all that different from you? I have heard that you people are unfriendly towards us and reject everything about us—the way we speak, how we look and what we eat. To you we are ugly, ungodly. Maybe you have always despised our beliefs and ways of living. Maybe we did something in the past to earn your enmity, but remember that you are in our territory right now. Accept that. Don't act foolishly in the forest. Keep your beliefs, if you must, but keep them to yourselves. As long as you are here, show the courtesy of respecting us. You may have heard horrible stories about us, but we, too, have heard similarly unflattering tales about you. Yet, *I* am not condemning you. It is not my way. Instead, I am inviting you to stay and offering my protection because you are clearly in need of it. Would an evil person do that? Why are you so afraid? I am not a yatudhani, born of a fire mantra, to kill rishis with my dark magic. Don't judge me without bothering to know me better.'

Her impassioned speech leaves them in shock. Kunti is the first to recover. 'We appreciate your honesty,' she says. 'But my son did kill your brother. How can we be safe in the forest that he ruled?'

'You imagine that I will blame you for his death? But that would not be fair. Hidimba had already decided that he was going to kill all of you, for no reason except to taste your flesh. Therefore, Vrikodar did the right thing by challenging and killing him. Every creature born of the earth acts according to its basic instinct. Life, without exception, is sacred for all. When threatened, to protect one's life, *by any means*, is thus every creature's duty. Whoever understands this knows how to act in a calamity. The biggest catastrophe is in hesitating to act…Hidimba was the one who attacked first. He was about to attack *me*. Vrikodar did not hesitate in coming to my defence. I am filled with admiration for his courage and prowess. I have no qualms about revealing my feelings—because they come from my heart. I also believe that, secretly, he returns them. I have never felt this way before about anyone, never seen any man look at me the way *he* did. I am certain that he and I are meant to be together. It is all I can think of, to have him for my mate.'

'That is your delusion,' says Kunti. 'You don't know him at all. You can only love those you know, those to whom you are connected.'

'But isn't true love about loving those you don't yet know? Isn't it about loving the whole world and not just those who are connected to you by kinship?'

Kunti's mouth is a straight thin line. 'Proposals of this nature are usually negotiated by one's family,' she says sharply. 'Have you sought the approval of your elders for this relationship? Don't you need to do that first?'

'But why would I need to do that first? Does a peacock seek his mother's permission before he dances for his mate? Does a lioness ask for her father's blessings before coupling with a lion? Mating is natural to all living creatures—when their bodies are ready for it. It involves only consent between a male and a female. I sense an equal desire in Vrikodar. My natural instinct is faultless.'

'That it is natural or faultless does not mean that it is also right. Your desire is inappropriate.'

'How can you say that? Happiness is the fruit of right action and what is right is also what follows the natural course. From the first moment I felt it in my body, my desire was as sharp and distinct as the other feelings I have: hunger, thirst, pain.'

'All animals have these feelings. However, *we* are not animals. The forest is not our natural home.'

Hidimbi looks at her, puzzled. 'Have you *never* felt what I feel now? How can that be? It means you have killed the part of you that is most alive.'

Her face stiff with anger, Kunti begins to walk away. Her sons follow her more slowly.

Hidimbi thinks of using a magic spell to keep them in the forest, but some inner compulsion prevents her. She takes a deep breath. There is only one more thing left for her to say. 'Please listen to me. I say this only out of concern for your welfare.'

They stop but do not look back.

'You are homeless and your lives are in danger. Fate has led you to the place that is the safest for you right now. You would be well-advised to stay on for some time. There is a lake at the edge of the forest. Go, bathe in it. On the opposite shore is Rishi Shalihotra's ashram. You will know it by the sacrificial fire that is always kept burning. The seer has lived in the ashram for many years. Through his tapasya he has obtained special powers that make the surrounding area a natural sanctuary. Hunters, bird-catchers, animal trappers and even those tribes that collect honey and gather herbs do not venture there. We rakshasas, too, leave the place alone. The rishi's presence is good for the forest. In our own way, we are grateful and keep an eye on the ashram. It is absolutely safe, as well as, a pleasant spot. Live there very quietly for some time. When it is no longer dangerous for you to leave, by all means go... no one will stop you.'

❖

After all they had been through, the lake is a cool slice of heaven. As they approach it, the sun's rays are burning off its misty cover, revealing the sparkle of emerald-green waters. Ducks and other water birds paddle among the bulrushes, pairs of leggy sarus cranes pick their way through the wet grass, foraging for worms. The air smells of damp, rich soil and the layered aromas of the forest.

Emerging from the bath, they find under a tree fresh sets of garments made of bark cloth.

'Are we to wear *these*?' Nakul asks, looking put off.

'They are appropriate for the forest,' Yudhisthir replies.

'Didn't I say that she was a yatudhani?' Bheem asks of no one in particular, more out of stubbornness than anything else. Barely has he spoken when a spread of fresh fruit materialises. 'It may not be safe to eat them,' he warns.

Arjun, about to break off a banana from a bunch, pauses. 'Will we turn into pigs?'

'That too has been known to happen,' Bheem says heavily.

Arjun is divided between his hunger and his misgivings. Hunger triumphs. He reaches for a banana. Peeling it, he wolfs it down with obvious relish.

'How does it taste?' asks Nakul, nervously watching him.

'How do you feel?' chimes in Sahadev.

'Restored,' replies Arjun, grinning. 'Ready for anything.' He reaches nonchalantly for a handful of jamun.

7

The Plan

As the day extricates itself from the bloody event of the night, its normal rhythms take over. Entering Shalihotra's ashram, the Pandavas are greeted by an oasis of order and ordinariness that seems surreal. There is no threat here, not even a hint. Instead, there is the calm but busy air of a veterinary hospital.

Bamboo enclosures hold several animals that are recuperating from surgery: a barking deer, a porcupine, a reptile, a civet cat. Peacocks stroll about, a pair of pelicans swim in a large pond, a spotted deer with one of its hind legs in stilts grazes under the trees. A few disciples, dressed in bark cloth, are sorting out freshly collected medicinal herbs. Two young men are holding down a monitor lizard, while a third, carefully avoiding its jaws, gingerly prods its chest. Two tribal children, a boy and his younger sister, the latter holding a sick baby monkey to her chest, wait patiently under a neem tree. The Pandavas and Kunti join them in waiting. An acolyte goes indoors to inform Shalihotra of the visitors. After several minutes, Yudhisthir is ushered into the rishi's private quarters to speak with him.

Sunburnt, of medium height and lean muscle, Shalihotra has a narrow, friendly face, crinkly eyes and the observant manner of a born healer. Yudhisthir offers him salutations. The rishi is a man of few words. 'I know who you people are,' he says without any preamble. 'I also know why you are in the forest.'

'We too have heard of you, Munivar,' Yudhisthir says, respectfully. 'Your work with wild animals is perhaps not as well-known as your expertise with horses. They say, in Aryavarta, that you are the last word on *that* subject.'

Shalihotra tilts his head, modestly acknowledging the compliment. 'You are safe here, Pandava, for as long as you wish to stay. We will make arrangements for you all to be comfortable.'

'Thank you, but living in the ashram would not be prudent for us, Munivar,' says Yudhisthir.

Shalihotra smiles wryly. 'Are you worried about the rakshasas? Hidimbi is the queen now. Compared to her brother, she is benign. If she has granted you protection, no one will touch a hair on your head.'

'That is reassuring, Munivar, but I wasn't referring to the rakshasas. There are other more malign forces against us.'

'I repeat, you are safe in the ashram. It's true that the kings and merchants of Aryavarta sometimes consult me, but they do not come *here*. I don't encourage it.'

'Nothing discourages a well-paid informer.'

The rishi looks thoughtful and nods but does not reply.

'We do not intend to stay here indefinitely,' says Yudhisthir. 'A few weeks at the most, till interest in the recent events dies down.'

Shalihotra slowly shakes his head. 'You will need to lie low for longer than that because of what happened last night in the forest. As the news of Hidimba's killing spreads, questions are bound to be asked.'

'Who will ask these questions?'

'For a start, other rakshasas who will certainly not be as friendly as Hidimbi. There are a few of them still alive. They stick to their territories, but visit cach other from time to time. Just to give you an idea of how effective the forest's communication methods are, there is a rumour that a nishadh woman and her five sons have been missing since the night of the fire.' Shalihotra's expression is deadpan.

'Is there any such talk in Varnavat too?'

'The talk there is all about the tragedy in Varnavat. There is a great deal of sympathy for the Pandavas and their mother. There is genuine sorrow as well. Pandu's sons were well-liked. The Varnavat folk blame Purochan because he built the house of lac—on Duryodhan's orders. His reputation, locally, was always a bit dubious. The people are saying that it is retribution that he too was burnt to death in the fire trap he created.'

Yudhisthir lets out a long sigh of relief.

'But there are murmurs of treachery everywhere,' says Shalihotra. 'Pandu's male line has been wiped out entirely, Dhritarashtra's sons have a free run. That kind of talk...There is also a rumour that an investigation into the burning incident may be ordered by none other than Bhishma himself. Apparently, he is most disturbed by the tragedy.'

He would be, thinks Yudhisthir. It happened on his watch. His network of spies covers every corner of Aryavarta. If they ask the right questions, they will, before long, discover the subterfuge.

'And the king?'

'Dhritarashtra is in mourning.'

❖

'Didn't I tell you?' says Bheem, furiously. 'Being the hypocrite that he is, our uncle pretends that he knows nothing. He imagines that by making a spectacle of his sorrow—a state mourning, a lavish funeral feast, generous donations to brahmins and visible displays of weeping—he will fool everyone.'

'It is possible that his grief is genuine,' says Yudhisthir, drily. 'We have no way of knowing how much he knows about the conspiracy to murder us—and we will never find out.'

Bheem curls his lip. 'You say this because you cannot bring yourself to believe that he is capable of such a grand deception.'

'I also say it because he is the king. Without solid proof we cannot accuse him of conniving in a plot to have us murdered. That is tantamount to treason and will not be well-received anywhere.'

Arjun interjects, 'I, too, feel a bit uneasy about it. Our uncle may favour Duryodhan, but no one can accuse him of callousness towards us. It is hard to imagine that he would play an active part in a plot to have his own kin killed. He has always shown that he respects dharma.'

'Hah!' scoffs Bheem. 'A king who is righteous himself but shuts his eyes to others who are not is a fraud. Worse, he uses his power unfairly. While we are on the subject, let me ask you this. Duryodhan too is a kshatriya, but did that stop him earlier from attempting a cold-blooded murder? I am speaking about the incident at Pramanakoti. Don't you remember what they did there? It may have been years ago, but *I* haven't forgotten. He and Shakuni poisoned *and* drowned me—to make doubly sure. If the nagas hadn't saved me…'

'Brother,' says Arjun, faintly mocking. 'Everything does not boil down to that old rivalry between Duryodhan and yourself.'

'Don't underestimate it, Brother,' retorts Bheem. '*That old rivalry* may have started as a personal animosity between the two of us back then, but when Duryodhan saw how I could singlehandedly thrash all his siblings, he recognised the threat I posed to his future…The first attempt to get rid of me failed, but with time the intention has become even more deadly because his lust for power, too, has grown.'

'This is mere conjecture.'

'Is it?' Bheem raises an eyebrow. 'How did it miss your attention, Arjun, that the legendary enmity is no longer only between Duryodhan and me? Think about it: *why* did he choose to befriend your rival Karna? Why did he openly ignore the rules and anoint that sutaputra as the king of Anga? Because he understood how anxious you were that no one should challenge your fame. The charioteer's son is the one *you* should worry about. Even Acharya Drona cannot cut him down to size now that he is Duryodhan's friend.'

Arjun scowls in response, but says nothing.

Bheem turns to Yudhisthir. '*You* told me to keep quiet about the Pramanakoti incident because I was the only victim at the time. But after we five defeated the king of Panchala and you were chosen as the yuvaraj, Duryodhan tried to have all of us burnt to death. What does that tell you? Isn't it a sign that his enmity is not restricted to me alone but includes Mother and all four of you too? Isn't it clear that he will rest only when every one of us is dead? Don't underestimate the risk he poses to you, specifically. Mark my words, the next time, he will go for *you* alone, and he will use the same trick, deception, to trap you…I know him…better than anyone else here.'

'We have gone over this many times in the past one year,' Yudhisthir says, wearily. 'Even if your opinion is right, what would you have me do?'

'End the problem *right now*! Left to me, I want nothing more than to beat the stuffing out of Duryodhan. It's what he deserves. In fact, why don't we return to Hastinapur after a few days?' Bheem laughs loudly. 'Their faces when we walk in will be worth the long journey.'

'I concur,' says Arjun. 'We should go back. Running away will not get us justice. In the presence of the entire court, the king cannot deny us what is ours.'

'We cannot go back,' Yudhisthir replies. 'That path is closed to us.'

'Why?'

'As Bheem has pointed out, the stakes have changed. With the tacit support of his father and the command of the treasury that he was given, Duryodhan has the resources. With his uncle Shakuni to help him as always, he will find some other way to get rid of us.'

'We can deal with that later,' says Bheem. 'You are the rightful heir. Stake your claim.'

Yudhisthir shakes his head. 'We cannot go back.'

'Why not? Are we are still trapped in the house of lac?' says Bheem. 'It seems to me that we are. Another year of pretending that everything is normal when it isn't.'

Yudhisthir smiles at him. 'I can't understand why you find it difficult. *I* don't have any problem. It makes sense to remain here. If there is, indeed, an investigation on the orders of Pitamaha, we should lie low till it's over.'

'But we left our weapons behind in the house of lac precisely for that reason,' says Nakul. 'Will that not be enough evidence to convince the investigators that those six bodies are the Pandavas and their mother?'

'It is a kind of proof, yes, but a good investigator will look for something more conclusive. There is one thing though: if they find human remains that are charred beyond recognition, Pitamaha may not be entirely convinced, but the king and the prime minister will want the enquiry ended, albeit for very different reasons.'

'And then?' Bheem's voice is deceptively calm. 'What happens after that? Are we going to wear these bark clothes for the rest of our lives? Are we going to remain outsiders everywhere we go? Is our fate to be refugees, dependent on others' goodwill for our very survival? Is that how you see us?' Yudhisthir does not reply. Goaded by his silence, Bheem says in a louder voice, 'This is not merely a temporary feint to fool our enemies, but a clean break from all that is rightfully ours. Why should we give it up without a fight?'

'We have given up nothing,' says Yudhisthir. 'However, staying alive is all that matters—for now. Duryodhan is powerful. His influence is widespread. He has everything in his favour to support his evil plan: position, allies and complete control of the treasury, not to forget the unspoken backing of his father. We saw that for ourselves at the games. Dhritarashtra overrode all protests when Duryodhan declared Karna as the king of Anga. On the other hand, we are in no position to fight. We have nothing right now.'

Bheem flexes his biceps. '*Strength* is the hallmark of a kshatriya.'

'Though it is what *you* prefer, violence is only one

form of strength. Right now, we need to follow the path of least resistance.'

'*Least* resistance! That is what brought us here—to a dead end.'

Yudhisthir shakes his head. 'It's an opportunity. We need to build new relationships that will allow us to emerge as ourselves.'

'And when will that happen?'

'I don't know, but happen it will.'

'We *are* already in a better position than we were a few days ago,' says Sahadev quietly. 'We have managed to deceive the deceivers. Our enemies believe we are dead.'

Bheem gives a snort of derision. 'If we play dead for too long, we will fade from public memory.'

'On the contrary, our task is cut out for us,' says Yudhisthir. 'For a start, we have to work on a shelter big enough for all of us. Rishi Shalihotra has suggested a secluded spot not far from the ashram. It is naturally well-guarded by thick trees and there is a small stream not far away.'

'For how long will we be in hiding? Or are you thinking of making this a lifelong retreat like our father did with Shatashringa forest?'

'We are not retreating, nor will we be in hiding… but we can try, for a while, to live inconspicuously. That means blending with the forest communities, making ourselves useful to them. Shalihotra mentioned that he could do with some assistance. Knowing how much Nakul and Sahadev love animals, I thought it would be a good thing if they helped out at the animal hospital.'

'Good thinking,' Arjun says. 'They can keep their ears to the ground. Mucking around the stables and cowsheds is perfect for picking up gossip. But I would like to remain outdoors.'

'We need to eat too,' says Yudhisthir. 'The surrounding forest is rich in game, herbs and berries. That's where you will go.'

'What role have you cast me in?' asks Bheem, still truculent.

For a moment, Yudhisthir looks at Bheem as if gauging him. 'Mother will surely have something in mind for you.'

8

A Mother's Wish

It is evening. Light filtering through the trees enters the clearing where the hut is under construction. In a few days it will be ready. Though the hour fosters tranquillity, a winding down, the air among the two who are standing inside the half-built dwelling is tense.

Of all her children, Kunti found Bheem the most difficult to deal with. Blessed with an overabundance of energy and brute strength, he had, in his early years, been a cheerful, gregarious child. But, she recalls, a change had come over him after Pandu's death; a new aggression had replaced his earlier sanguine nature. Maybe it was the move to Hastinapur, the overcrowded conditions in the palace and the difficulty of adapting to new faces and a vastly different lifestyle that had made him restive, belligerent and hot-tempered. She hadn't thought much about it then as the new life had required so many adjustments of her as well. Besides, with her and his brothers, he had always been the same person—frank, affectionate and trustworthy. Beneath the rough exterior, she knew implicitly, was a curiously childlike nature, a sensitive caring heart that beat only to protect his family. Studying his grim face now, she thinks a mother must learn to speak in many different languages.

'Treat it as my wish,' she says, gently. 'Marry Hidimbi.'

'Can't you wish for something simpler? Like inviting me to tie a rope to a tree-branch, make a noose from the loose end and hang myself...I do believe that I could manage that much.'

Unperturbed, Kunti says, 'Yudhisthir, too, thinks that it is the proper thing to do.'

'As propriety matters so much to him, why doesn't *he* marry her?'

Kunti clicks her tongue. 'Show some respect! What Pandu once was to you, so is your elder brother now. You must defer to him.'

'But I do! Since he comes ahead of me, he should be the first to marry. I am surprised that being the stickler for norms and rules that he is, he has overlooked this very important dictate of tradition...Or is she unsuitable for him but not for me? Is that it?'

Kunti shakes her head. 'It's not that,' she says. 'Her eyes see only you. It is you her heart is set on. She has approached Yudhisthir only because she believes you will not ignore his wishes.'

'But you just said that it was *your* wish. Did she come to you too? *Again? After* you had refused? Doesn't she recognise that a no means *no*?'

Kunti sends him a reproving look. After a while, she says quietly, 'Yes, she revealed her heart to me. Her feelings are genuine. I could not help but feel sorry. She is a woman in love, pining for you. She said that she will die without you…Respect her desire.'

'Which just happens to be your desire as well as Yudhisthir's. I find it too contrived to be a mere coincidence. Speak your mind, Mother. You never do anything without a good reason. Why are you ordering me to marry a lowborn creature like Hidimbi?'

'Don't use that tone for her. It is belittling.'

'*Belittling!* She's a rakshasi and not to be trusted. Who knows when she may reveal her true colours and murder us all in our sleep? Don't allow her to get any closer to us.'

'Son, try to understand. I have studied her carefully. Her true colours arc what you see…Her nature is not as devious as you imagine, nor is she as aggressive as others of her race. Maybe it was the influence of her only male relative, her brother, who dominated her from her childhood, but she is surprisingly easy to control. We would not be able to survive in this place without her support. She has helped us a lot.'

'I agree. You have taught us never to disrespect those who serve us. But surely there must be a simpler way to show gratitude. Won't saying 'thank you' do?'

'Be serious!' says Kunti in a scolding tone. 'She has worked day and night beside you to build this dwelling for us. It's not only the heavy lifting that she helps with, but she also brings us gifts of fruit, berries, herbs and game whenever she comes by.'

'Which is every day,' Bheem says sourly.

'Oh!' Kunti sends him an arch look. 'So, you did notice that.'

He sighs. 'I'm not blind, Mother. It is hard to avoid looking at her. She shows up…*everywhere.*'

❖

He comes across her every day, is secretly flattered by her efforts to get his attention but continues to ignore her. Yet, every time he sees her, he is mesmerised. In daylight, with the others constantly present, snatched glances and sidelong looks are all that he permits himself; he knows no other way to escape the sly but constant teasing from his brothers. However, night, which brings oblivion to others, brings to him a different awakening. In sleep, the constraints between the thinkable and the unthinkable give way. The silent exchanges of daytime bleed into his dreams. The longing for her spreads through him like crimson light entering a lake at dawn, reflecting a brief hidden beauty. A yearning that his body knows only too well, from earlier encounters with women, shimmers in that tenuous half-light and dissolves. Though the forbidden beckons—with a wink, a playful nudge—he balks. It is familiar but still ambiguous. She is like every woman from whom he has sought pleasure. He experiences the same clandestine thrill, the curiosity and the same hot passion, but it is tempered by an inexplicable uneasiness. You are mine, she says, turning her face up towards him so that he can look into her eyes. Do they conceal deceit? Those arms that reach out for him appear like the tentacles of a monster. He turns away, sickened by the sham and shame her brazen looks make him feel. He runs, his ears ringing with her sorrowful cry, *All I want is to love you.* Runs from her arms that follow him or runs towards them, he cannot say. At this point, he wakes up thrashing about, heart thumping wildly in his chest. The dreams leave him feeling ill at ease, dissatisfied with himself, angry at the world, and strangely heavy-hearted. She is more than temptation; she is a craving, a quagmire, but is that her only pull? Is it she who calls out to him, or is it his own soul that screams to join her? Who is he when he is with her: a sleepwalker, an insomniac, a trapped man or a free one?

The return to daylight and the quotidian existence—the humble thatched roof and mud walls of their temporary housing, the unshaven faces, brawny bodies of his siblings, their horseplay and the rough and ready jokes, the sight of his mother struggling to get the kitchen fire going—brews in him a mix of both relief and apathy. As life reclaims him, bitterness and anger too regain energy; his natural aggression crushes the kingdom of dreams, turning her to dirt, turning everything about their dream life to dust.

Yet, were it not for the longing, were it not for the dreams, he would not be able to bear it.

❖

'She comes here because she continues to believe you like her,' says Kunti. 'Despite your explicit rudeness.' She notices that, this time, he looks a bit sheepish.

'It's not that simple,' he says, after a while. 'We are fugitives now, but we will not be like this forever. Yudhisthir has said that when the time is right, we will return to our old life. You want me to make her my wife, but tell me, Mother, how is it even possible? Do you see her fitting in with our kind of people?'

'Not for a minute.'

'What then?'

'What then? Tell me, Son, what do *you* foresee?'

He realises that the question is important to her.

War. When were we not thinking of it? Was there such a time? Maybe before we went to live in Hastinapur. But once we arrived there, we faced hostility every day. The childish heckling, the silly taunts during the games and in the friendly contests were only a precursor to the silent conspiracies of the future. Only Duryodhan and I, we who recognised each as the other, sensed how deadly a game we were playing. There was murder in our hearts even then. All that has changed since those days is that, with Dhritarashtra's protection, Duryodhan thinks he can outflank us...But it's only a matter of time before he and his evil plans are laid to rest for ever.

Aware that Kunti is waiting for a reply, he decides not to mince his words. 'Duryodhan is ready to go to any lengths to take away our father's kingdom from us. His jealousy knows no bounds. He will not rest till we are *wiped out.* As for me—what I dream about is the sweetness of giving back. Only when I have avenged the wrong done to us by Dhritarashtra and his sons, and restored what is rightfully ours, will I rest. Duryodhan wanted to kill us by treachery. He will pay for it. To answer your question, Mother, I foresee a struggle.'

'Then shouldn't you spend every moment preparing

for it?' she says calmly. 'A son born of you and Hidimbi will be a useful ally. Rakshasa blood will strengthen your side.'

He sends her a look of disbelief. '*Mother!* This is hardly the time or place for you to be planning grandchildren.'

'Think of it as a military alliance.'

He looks at her with an odd expression. 'Hmm... you and Yudhisthir seem to have it all worked out, as usual, down to the final battle plans.'

'But didn't you just say that you want nothing more than to avenge the wrongs done to us? A son will help you do that.'

He is surprised. The language of revenge has never been hers, but now it flows naturally. She has, he realises, become a mystery to him. Maybe she always was...Till this moment, he has not thought of her as anyone other than the mother he shared with his siblings. Always restrained in her demonstration of affection, she has, ever since their father's death, been more of a mentor than a mother. Strict but impartial, honest and just, she is the same with each of them. Yet, he senses for the first time that some deeper current has shifted in her. He cannot be more precise, but he is certain that something has changed recently—after the fire. She is not the same person any more. A new determination or maybe a new understanding has come to her. Only that would explain this illogical demand and this absurd conversation.

'And what of the wrong that will be done to him, this creature—this imaginary son of mine?' he asks in a parrying tone. 'Would I not have an obligation to him? Is it fair to choose his destiny for him even before his conception?'

'Pandu chose yours as he did those of your brothers. Kshatriyas resort to niyoga for a good reason. They need sons who can be their swords and shields. Each one of you is the gift of a certain god—*for a reason.*'

His face is stormy. The circumstances surrounding his birth, like those of his brothers, are known to him, but being reminded of them brings back other unpleasant memories from the years in Hastinapur. He makes one more attempt to make her change her mind. 'Is that all he will mean to you, your own grandson—a human mace to be wielded against our enemies?'

'*You* spoke of your duty,' she points out. 'But do you realise that duty cannot be interpreted as a single unambiguous commandment carved in stone? It does not apply equally in all situations. One can end up doing the wrong thing but for the right reason, just as one can do its opposite too. It means that one frequently has to make a choice of what or who needs to be sacrificed. A kshatriya cannot allow anything—inner contradictions, blood ties—to weaken him or hold him back from fulfilling his responsibility. If he fails, our society itself will collapse into chaos and we, ourselves, will cease to exist. The determination and clarity Pandu showed on the battlefield was absent in his life as king because his elder brother overshadowed him. He could never rid himself of the notion that the crown should have gone to Dhritarashtra, but for a point of law that was cited to deprive him of it. Dhritarashtra was naturally disappointed, but Pandu secretly blamed himself. Though he said that he was leaving the kingdom because he had been cursed for an error of judgement while hunting, *I* believe that his self-disgust was behind his decision to leave so abruptly. It was a bit drastic, even at that time, but remorse makes one do strange things. By letting go of the kingship of Hastinapur, Pandu imagined that he had—rightly or wrongly—corrected the injustice done to his elder brother. My assumption may not be entirely true, but isn't his abandoning his duty the reason why we are in these circumstances today? So how are his actions to be understood?'

Bheem watches her intently but says nothing.

She sighs tiredly. 'These are mere speculations. He has been gone a long time and I can only guess at his motives, but I have always wondered about his inordinate desire for sons. Pandu did not want just one or two, but as many as were possible. Sons are a warrior's strength; he can never have enough sons. But having given up his kingdom *why* did Pandu anticipate a war? Was it because he sensed that Dhritarashtra would not be satisfied with just being the regent? At that time, he said the sages had forecast a great future for his sons. Everyone knows that glory for a kshatriya comes from the battlefield. Your father's family tradition *is* your tradition too…Our life in Shatashringa forest was idyllic, but even then we realised that one cannot go on without thinking of the future. Pandu had started talking of returning to Hastinapur so that you five boys could be trained in your family's customs and rituals when he passed away.' She falls silent for a while and then says with greater urgency. 'There has to be more robustness in you, Bheem. A deeper hunger, a clearer sense of purpose. The feeling to act must rise in your heart. Only then there will be a roar, a flood in your veins. And only then will you come up with a realistic plan and start working on it. How else will anything change? You cannot hesitate to spill blood, even if it is your own.'

'*My* blood?' Bheem gives a mirthless laugh. 'What is it? Where does it come from? *Who am I*?' He breaks off, as if to calm himself and shakes his head slowly from side to side. 'I don't ask these questions, Mother. I *never* ask because I don't think I would comprehend the answer…Besides, how does it matter? We are what you have made us.' He meets her eyes reluctantly, revealing his own sense of bewilderment. 'After Father died in Shatashringa forest, you told us that Hastinapur was our home and the Kuru clan our family. You took us to live with them. However, from the day we entered the palace, we began to learn a new lesson in how families can be very different from our own. We tried to connect with our cousins, but from the start they treated us like imposters. Not only were they condescending, they mocked and bullied us too, because their number was much bigger. These very questions about our blood were flung at us brothers in insidious ways. Duryodhan flatly refused to see us too as the Kauravas, the descendants of Kuru. He didn't even call us the Pandavas. He would address us three as Kaunteyas, Kunti's boys, and Nakul and Sahadev as Madreyas.'

'You *are* a Kuntiputra…what was amiss?' Kunti asks with a frown.

'Did you ever make that distinction?'

She sends him a quizzical look. 'No. But aren't you making too much of trivial issues?'

He looks sheepish. 'On the surface there was nothing amiss, but I saw it as a veiled insult. I may have been overly sensitive and formed a wrong impression, but the sense I got was that it was one of his ways of rubbing it in that we were not related to them and had no right to live in the palace. I could have borne the daily harassment, but this sly way of repudiating our place in the Kuru lineage, and the implied questioning of our origin, made me wild with anger...Other than beating up those useless sons of Dhritarashtra, who had appropriated the family name Kauravas as if they alone had the right to it, I could do nothing. It made me so furious that even Yudhisthir could not keep me in check. It was petty to squabble over these matters, he said. Royal families *have* variegated lineages. They are like the powerful ocean into which many different streams merge. It was more important to maintain an equilibrium between all the contradictions so that the family remains stable.'

'He was correct...I was—*I am*—a queen of the Kurus, Son. That gave you every right to be there.'

'That too was what Yudhisthir said. As you were both our father and mother, Kuntiputra was our identity. *Your* word was the highest truth that we had to uphold... this was what he has said, time and time again. In that world, where men, like Pitamaha, Acharya Drona and Dhritarashtra, are in control, Yudhisthir taught us to see *you* as our strength. You keep us all together, Mother, and I respect that, but we still have to return to that world one day. To its conformism, its hierarchy, its innate belief that one's birth and bloodline decide nearly everything about one's life. The stories about our great-grandmother Satyavati and her lowly origins are muted now but they remain alive in the local gossip. Her reputation—'

She sends him a stern look, cutting him short mid-sentence. 'When it comes to scurrilous gossip, you have always been too sensitive. Develop a head for it, Son. Hierarchy exists in one's head alone. Though it is imaginary, its impact is real because it decides who matters and who does not...Dhritarashtra rules a kingdom he cannot see. He has encouraged his son to live in a fantasy too. Fantasies are fragile, but those who live them will go to any lengths to preserve them, including creating artificial divisions based on names. Nobody can reject your paternity or deny that Yudhisthir, the first son of Pandu, is also the firstborn in the new generation of the Kuru family; *he* is the eldest grandson of Vichitravirya. However, it should not be—and *it is not*—the only reason why Yudhisthir's claim is stronger than Duryodhan's. Your elder brother has shown himself worthy. The people see it, wise elders like Acharya Drona, Pitamaha Bhishma and Vidur accept it and Dhritarashtra too could not find a single reason to object to his appointment as yuvaraj.

Yudhisthir has a clear understanding of dharma. He will be a virtuous king but righteousness needs might to support it, or nothing will change for the better. It has become abundantly clear to me that you five will have to claim your patrimony through your own energy and effort. The times ahead will not be easy for you. You must plan…'

'I understand your meaning, Mother. We have to establish our own dynasty, which will be distinct. We have to be seen as virtuous as our father was. But, if I marry Hidimbi, Aryavarta will not see it as a respectable match. Royal families look down on rakshasa women for their boldness and free ways of living. They regard them as evil personified. Neither Hidimbi nor her son will have a shred of legitimacy or respect among kshatriyas. He will be treated with the contempt reserved for a half-breed, yet full loyalty is what *we* will expect of him. You spoke of a military alliance. It reminds me of the relationship between Karna and Duryodhan who befriended the sutaputra only because he saw the possibility of winning against us. Though the charioteer's son is now Duryodhan's closest friend and has been elevated in status, many kshatriyas still give him a wide berth. I, too, can't help but feel that he doesn't deserve to be in our company. He doesn't know how to be among us. His place is in the stables and not in the sabha where he now sits…'

It is suddenly very quiet in the room. His eyes flicker to her face.

'Do you want me to be responsible for my son's pain?' he asks.

She appears calm but a vein throbs in her temple. Her thoughts are far away.

We bring them into the world in pain. And pain is all the world gives them. A child of Surya, born for power, victory and fame, a king now in his own right, yet all he will be known as is that sutaputra Karna. *Guilt. I know what it feels like. One is never completely free of it. It lodges itself deep in your bones. Even if you can't see it, it's there. Tear it out of its hiding place. Throw it away. Walk away from it. Or do nothing and let it remain…but* never, under any circumstance, *repeat the act that brought it on in the first place. Do not become an oppressor while you also see yourself as the victim. Else your judgement will be flawed, your cruelty will know no bounds.*

'That is why I am asking you to marry her,' she says evenly. 'To give her son *your* name so that he knows who his father is. His famous father. Knowing that he has royal blood in him will motivate him to work for our welfare. Mahamantri Vidur, as everyone knows, is a dasiputra. He is loyal to the Kurus and has always worked in their interest.'

'Yet Duryodhan has no regard for him.'

'Even if you marry Hidimbi, it will be only for a

year, in any case,' she says, with a slight hesitation in her voice.

'For a year!' His mouth falls open.

'It doesn't take longer for a baby to be born…You will have time with her till then, but we must leave the forest soon after that. Naturally, she will not leave with us.' Her tone implies that a year is long enough for the proposed relationship to run its natural course.

Though his tone is still respectful, his eyes are hard. 'Mother, you, who prizes constancy above all, are asking me to take a woman for one year as my wife. You want me to do this for the sole purpose of getting a son who will fight on our side—one day. But what of the woman herself?'

'What about her?'

'How can it be right for me to leave the mother of my son to bring him up alone? Is my name the only thing I will leave him?'

'You forget that it is the most valuable legacy a man leaves his son.' She meets his gaze squarely. 'Pandu, too, left you only his name.'

'Not true, Mother. He left us a dream, we have to get his kingdom back.'

She takes a deep breath and lets it out slowly. 'You have answered your own question, Son. Your first obligation is to your dead father, to me and to your brothers. That is a higher dharma than any other. In fulfilling *this* commitment lies the special destiny you were born to attain.'

'But I cannot ignore the second commitment entirely. As a husband, a man has a duty to his wife.'

'You will fulfil that by giving her a son. Bheem, listen to me carefully. Attachment, passion—these are bonds that tie a warrior down. They should not cloud your thinking. Choose the path that is right for you. Will you be able to live with yourself if you abandon *us*?'

'Isn't it also shameful for a man to abandon his wife and child?'

'When it is clear to everyone but him that the child cannot be his heir, then how is it shameful?' Kunti counters sharply. Mellowing her tone, she continues, 'Such agreements as the one I'm proposing are not uncommon when men have to travel away from their native places for a length of time. It's entirely natural to feel desire, but like the flowers that bloom for a season and fade away, romance too has a limited role. You are young, hot-blooded...Though you try to disguise your feelings for her, they are obvious to everyone. Fortunately for you, we are in a different place now, the mores here allow for a different arrangement. Men and women mingle freely. These women have the freedom to be with more than one man. They are not judged for it. Hence, as long as your relationship stays within the forest, it is *not* wrong or shameful. She will not suffer a loss of reputation and neither will your son. I have thought about it carefully...You will not have to worry about abandoning them to an uncertain fate. Rakshasa children grow up much faster than us. As she has no other close male relative, your son will be the heir to his mother's kingdom. Just as they have no place in Hastinapur, *you* have no place here. It's only a sojourn for you. Hidimbi understands this because short-term relationships are not uncommon here. Thus, her expectations from you are limited. She and her son will have each other and this forest, which is their natural home. If you really care about her well-being at all, you must accept that this is where she and her son are likely to be most at ease...Don't anticipate that she will be ready to leave it for you. It is an interlude, nothing more, in Hidimbi's life. There will be someone else to take your place later, just as there will be other women in your life...Why should she mean anything more to you?'

'That does not answer *my* question, Mother.'

'It is important to see the limits in one's life, Son. Instead of asking me the question, ask yourself a more pertinent one: what is your dharma? Is your life going to be that of a warrior or that of a forest-dweller? You are at a crossroads. You have to choose one of the two, but it has to be quick.'

He turns his back to her and stares into the growing darkness. The site they have chosen for their hut is in a dense part of the forest. Access to it is not simple, but the feeling that they are in grave danger remains. When night falls, the surroundings lose their normality and acquire a more sinister look. The thicket grows dense, trails narrow but seem to gain more branches that loop in on themselves. One may abandon a path for another, but at the end of the day, it doubles back to the same place.

We have been reduced to this. We call ourselves noble but we are, in fact, exiles everywhere we go. Trapped in a void, we don't even know in which direction we should go. Yet, we must remain committed to the dharma we were born into because it reminds us of our place in the only world we know. Even though we live outside *that world now, we are not free of it. It remains relevant to every moment of our life. We can never become anything else other than what we are born to be. A strong fence and a strong door against outsiders, a hierarchy in our heads. Inside. Outside. Our world, their world. Our lives, their lives. Bheem can pretend to be a forest-dweller, but he cannot become one. He can sire a child but he cannot be a real father to that child. He is a kshatriya, she is a rakshasi. A mating is all that is possible…But I am—aren't we all?—something more than the role assigned by birth. Must* everything *be decided for me? Yet, even I…I don't know what to do. Yes, I want Hidimbi, but why does it have to be only on these terms? To call it a marriage is one thing, but is it a marriage? Why think about it so much? Why lie to myself? Can't I admit that I don't own myself? Without her, I would be able to live, but without my family—no, I cannot dream of it. Mother is right as always. We are lost now, but we will find our way back to the life that is ours—the only life possible for us. A rakshasi cannot be a Pandava queen…I want her body, I do not want her. And a temporary marriage is the perfect solution. Allow it to happen. Just go with it. It's a simple solution to everyone's problems.*

As if realising that he is mulling too much, Kunti sends him an impatient look. 'What is your answer, Son? What should I say to her?'

His jaw tightens. The blood inside him beats loud enough to deafen him. He knows that something more is being asked of him than is fair. The price will be extracted from him alone, it may diminish him in his own eyes but that will be a judgement made in the secret recess of his heart. Anything is justifiable when it is in the larger interests of the family.

'Tell her whatever you think fit,' he says roughly and leaves the place.

9

The Bride's Day

'So that's the sum of it then,' says Vichitra. 'You get Vrikodar for one year and they get the lifetime services of an invincible warrior.'

Hidimbi is silent, remembering the recent conversation with Kunti and Yudhisthir. Bheem was present too, but he had played no part in it. All three had maintained a guarded stance. It had reminded her of the high, sharp-pointed barrier she had been told to put up around their hut. The task of building it had been easy, but it had seemed unfriendly to her.

'Of course, you agreed *immediately*,' prompts Vichitra, throwing her a reproving look.

Even when they speak nicely, as they always do, they make me feel left out. My presence is an intrusion they put up with because they have no choice. Why? What have I missed out in my effort to make them comfortable? I get the feeling that I must learn to shrink and be less noticeable when I stand before them.

Hidimbi shakes her head. 'Not immediately. I asked whether the second condition would apply to a baby girl too?'

Vichitra chuckles. 'And?'

'They did not bother to reply and spoke instead of the wedding ceremony.'

'A ceremony for an arrangement meant for *one* year? Why go through the trouble?'

'Mata Kunti was adamant about it.'

'*Mata?*'

'That is the respectful way to address her I was told.' Hidimbi rolls her eyes. 'She said that it was in my interest as it would make an honourable woman of me. Whatever that is.'

'What did you say?'

'That it still wasn't necessary—because *we* honour every woman equally and no less than every man. I asked her if it was different among the Aryas.'

'*Really?*' Vichitra's lips curve in a mischievous smile.

Hidimbi shoots her a puzzled look. '*Was* it such a strange question? Vrikodar gave a snort of amusement when he heard it, but he quickly looked away. His elder brother looked surprised and slightly disapproving, as if I'd said something odd. As for Mata Kunti, she just pretended she hadn't heard me. She pursed her lips.

It makes her look strange—like she has no mouth. For some reason, she does it quite often when I am around.'

'Did anyone care to answer your question?'

'Her elder son did, though he sounded a bit flustered, waffling about the Aryas honouring married women, *wives and mothers*, above others. They wanted to honour me, he said, in their own way. As the new queen of the rakshasas, it was only right that I should be given due respect. The son born of the union would be the next king of the rakshasas.'

'And their ally…How convenient!' murmurs Vichitra. A look of scorn narrows her eyes. 'Not good enough to be recognised openly as a grandson, but at their beck and call when they need a strong man to fight their wars. Is this what you want, Hidimbi? More importantly, is it what you want for your son? Are you prepared to give his power to another tribe?'

'I…I didn't think of it that way…I haven't thought that far. I *don't* want to think about it. I just want to be with Vrikodar. For a night, a month of nights, six months, a year, I don't care! I'm not thinking of how much time we will have, only of ways to make it beautiful. Our time together is so little, anyway, I want our hours to be a celebration of all the happiness being with him gives me. There are so many places I want to show him. For them, the forest is filled with terrors.

I want him to see it as a haven. If he realizes that the forest is the safest place for them, that he can be happy here, he may want to make the year-long marriage into a longer one.'

'That wasn't my question.'

'I would be happy to give birth to his son—or daughter. I would want the child to know its father and not just know *about* him. When they said that they would not remain here beyond a year, I offered to leave too and go wherever they wanted with them. I want to see the world, I said. For some reason, none of them thought it was a good idea. The elder son Yudhisthir said something about their nomadic life being inconvenient and their need for anonymity. I tried to say that I can assume different forms at will, but I could see that their minds could not comprehend that. So, I gave them a demonstration of shape-shifting.'

'*You did*?'

'Uhn…hunh. It wasn't a full moon, my powers were not at their peak. It was a small act, really.'

'The blue butterfly? Or were you the singing bird? The stinging bee?'

'A golden deer.'

Vichitra's jaw falls open. 'Don't tell me! The last time a rakshasa turned into a golden deer, he ended up with an arrow through his heart.'

'It's an act I have always wanted to try out, but before the right audience. I thought that as they were Aryas, it would impress them...but they looked quite shaken.'

'And why not? It led to a terrible war the last time.'

'Well, this time it won't. They made it clear that Vrikodar could have nothing to do with me once he left the forest. Then why will they want anything to do with my son?'

'Is that what Vrikodar too wants—to have nothing to do with *his* son?'

'He didn't say a word to make me believe differently.'

'Does it seem fair?'

Hidimbi chews a corner of her lower lip. 'Strangely, it does. I have thought about it...it is fair. Marriage is not a pre-condition to pairing off. It happens by mutual consent, is not exclusive and need not even be permanent. But Mata Kunti said that in their world, such a relationship is not permitted. Marriage is a duty, she said.' Adopting Kunti's calm but austere manner, she mimics her dry, flat tone perfectly. '*Giving birth to a son is your duty too. It is nothing more, or less, than what is expected from all married women in our society.*'

'*Motherhood*,' says Vichitra, with an ironic twist to her mouth. 'How they *exalt* it! You do understand what this means, don't you? Mata Kunti cannot be disobeyed. For the one year that you are married to Vrikodar, he—and his mother—will have exclusive rights over you…That is why they are insisting on a marriage.'

Hidimbi looks at Vichitra worriedly. '*Complete rights.* What does that mean?'

'As the daughter-in-law, you are their property for a year and your son is bonded to them for life.'

For a while Hidimbi is silent. 'These conditions don't bother me,' she says with a toss of her head. 'I can take care of myself and my child till he is old enough to fend for himself. That is what mothers do anyway. What puzzles me is how often they used some words, *expect, respect*…The elder brother asked me if I understood what was expected of me. He wanted to know if I would respect all the terms of the arrangement.'

'What terms?' Vichitra's tone is sharp.

'The first is that Vrikodar and I can spend the daylight hours together, but he must return to them at nightfall. He must sleep under their roof.'

'How bizarre!' says Vichitra. After a few moments, she adds, 'This is not a term but a precaution. They want him penned in for the night—like cattle. And you? Even before you exhibited your ability to change shape, they would have assumed that rakshasas do precisely that so that they can do their foraging at night. Do they intend to let you range across the countryside drinking blood, killing babies and seducing young males—or whatever they imagine of you? What about *your* sleeping arrangements?'

'I am to sleep in Mata Kunti's hut.'

A resounding silence followed by a deep sigh. 'Just as I suspected—she means to cage you as well.'

Hidimbi lowers her head. 'I agreed…to everything.'

Vichitra clicks her tongue to show her disapproval. 'Girl, what were you even thinking? A rakshasi bows to no one. How could you forget that? Why have you agreed to *their* norms? Why did you not remind them that *they* are in the forest now and they could try showing respect to the custom here? Vrikodar is the one who should move out of his family and move in with you.'

'He is devoted to his family in a way I have never seen before. I don't think that he would ever be comfortable not living with them. He is very protective.' Hidimbi cannot bring herself to repeat Kunti's actual words: *Bheem's first duty is to take care of us, his family. It is a difficult time for us. He cannot indulge in long, leisurely dalliances with you. Nor can he ever leave us for you.* 'Their own relatives want them dead,' she says abruptly. 'Their lives are in great danger!'

'How can their lives be in danger when the entire forest is under your protection? For them, there is *no* place safer than this one. *You* are all powerful here.'

'Am I? I am not as sure of my power if I cannot have him. You think that it was foolish of me to give in, but I want him—on any terms.'

'Then you should have eaten him when you had the power *and* the chance,' says Vichitra, acidly. 'That would have been more satisfying.'

'He is different, I admit, now that I know them a little better, but I can't see him that way, as separate.'

'That is the trouble with you. You don't *want* to see…why?'

Why? Because he is perfect for me. Though their encounter is bound to be short, she knows she can never forget him. She does not want to spend the rest of her nights sleepless in her tree-house thinking of him and wondering how it would be if he had kissed her. She wants a different memory: of being kissed and touched, of kissing and touching him. She knows that he too wants her equally. The forest has wrought its magic on him and his senses are alive in a new way. When she looks into his eyes, every other language loses meaning, but this wordless one. It is natural to feel this way, she tells herself, to feel that a mere glance from him is enough for her to lose herself. The one thing, the only thing of significance in all of creation, is for them to come together. They are meant for each other just as the sky and the earth together form all life.

'I also have the feeling that Vrikodar takes a dim view of this whole scheme.'

'He probably realises that it's stupid and backward,' says Vichitra. 'But he is not willing to follow his heart the way you are. He too believes that his family's interest must take precedence over his own. That should tell you something about what to expect from your relationship with him.'

'Has his heart room for only them and none for me?' Hidimbi shakes her head. 'I don't think so...I know it in my bones that it's just Mata Kunti and his elder brother who keep him back. He is the strongest of them all, yet he tamely submits to their will. I cannot understand his fear.'

'What fear?'

'I don't know. It stems from Mata Kunti. She isn't easy to read. She is a constant presence around them, quiet and composed, but also watchful, alert to the smallest sign of danger. At first, I thought it was because she was inexperienced in forest life, but it's clearly not that. She knows our way of life.'

'Then it's more likely to do with you. She is the mother of *five* virile sons. That would explain the twitchiness.'

'She needn't worry. I want only Vrikodar.'

Vichitra makes a face. 'I simply cannot understand

your fascination for him. You've lived quite happily till now—*without* him. Then why do you feel this all-consuming passion, this need that he has to be a part of your existence?'

'I don't honestly know…I've asked myself that too. There was something different from the very beginning. I felt a sense of awe. Ever since then, I have seen him so many times…I still feel it. As if I'm in the presence of someone special…I can't think straight. He is unlike every other male I've known. Not just good-looking, but with real goodness within. He is strong and fearless. He fought Hidimba to save his family. Doesn't that tell *you* something about him? He alone is stronger than all his brothers. That is why his mother relies on him.'

'A rakshasi relies on no one but herself. Remember that.'

'A rakshasi, as you said, is not respected by them. But they all treat Mata Kunti with dignity. Amongst themselves they bicker and banter, but with her they are respectful and gentle. They never do anything without consulting her…To be honest, I find it odd. Anyway, to answer your question, I want him in my life *because* he is so different. When I am near him, I see that it is possible for me, too, to be a different person. I want to be that woman—the kind of woman he would *want* to love.'

'*Winning* a man's love is hard work,' says Vichitra, drily.

'You misunderstand! It's not about winning or losing.' She breaks off, unable to find the right words to express herself. After a while, she says, 'My brother used to make me feel like a loser. With Vrikodar, I feel the opposite. I *know* how he makes me feel—as if I am special. There is a glow in his eyes when he sees me. *I feel it on my skin.* An aliveness. There is nothing false about it.'

Vichitra shakes her head slowly. 'You think you've fallen in love, *but* all you have fallen into is a...well.'

'Then let me drown!'

'Spoken like a true hostage. Love has taken you too, just like it took your mother. Same choice, same destiny. Caused by the same imbalance of desires. You desire him more than is good for you and *he*—he desires you too little.'

'Please...don't say that!'

'Probably the same tears too. Silly girl! You are binding yourself hand and foot. You *will* drown. When is the wedding to be?'

'Tomorrow. A small, private ceremony at the new house. Very quiet.'

❖

Quiet it is not.

The day unfurls, like a flower to the sun, with a dawn of exceptional beauty. A majestic sky, washed clean by a shower, hangs above, soft as the finest muslin bridal shawl and just as luminous. The forest is a newly painted mansion. Millions of blooms, pink, red and auspicious yellow, garland its passageways; in its quiet niches, colourful butterflies sway delicately like oil lamps. The grass is a chequered carpet of many different greens. Sunbeams slide into the darkest corners, bringing in the sweetness of light, the lightness of fragranced airs, wild jasmine everywhere. Velvet notes fly out of the bulbul's syrinx in a newly minted paean to an impossible love; langurs rehearse cartwheels and somersaults, peacocks, proud-eyed, lead a shimmering rally of feathers. The breeze, not to be outdone, dances the leaves in gentle dervish swirls. And yet there is a melancholy underlying the festivity, the pensiveness of goodbyes unspoken. The trees sing the wedding songs. Hidimbi's own shala clings to her in the deepest embrace, weeping quiet tears as it heaps blessings on her and promises to keep her tree-house clean and ready. She will return, won't she?

And the gifts keep arriving: the clouds deliver a drizzle, each drop gold-tipped by the sun. The new bride bathes under an arch of rainbows. Dewdrop pendants for her ears, a turquoise feather for her hair, jokes to make her laugh away the nervousness. Dressed in yellow-dyed bark skin, with a beaded circlet atop her head, her skin lustrous as a lily, her hair, long, loose and flower-scented. She stands on the highest branch of her home in the shala tree for the last time, a graceful bride, stretches her arms and sails into the air, across the forest, towards a new life.

❖

Kunti is in a thoughtful mood. A wedding is auspicious, a portal to a family's future. But weddings, in her experience, have turned out very differently: they lead you into blind alleys and forsaken hopes. Her own had led her to Hastinapur.

Memory wings her back to her first sight of the high brick walls of the fabled city, the soft light of the cow dust hour, the gilded domes and the grand welcome that had awaited her, the queen. Bells pealed as the chariot wheels rolled through the streets and under the flower arches, past the crossroads decorated with tall lamps. The sound of conches filled the air. It had been a new beginning. How trusting she was then, how hopeful. How naïve. Hastinapur was to teach her better. Every day brought a fresh lesson, usually a hard one. Yet the hardest had been leaving Hastinapur. Home. Kingdom. The cheering still rings in her ears, rings true with not a single false note.

She wipes the memories away and turns to the bride,

her first daughter-in-law, with a warm smile.

'A simple exchange of garlands,' she says. 'Followed by a meal, which you will cook and serve.'

'I? Cook?'

'Why not? Don't you know how to? You'll have to learn.'

'I do know how to cook, but *today*?'

'It's customary,' Kunti explains in her dry, patient way. 'The ritual of lighting the kitchen fire for the first time. I will help you, of course, with the cooking—just for today. Nothing too fussy, but the sooner you learn our ways the better.'

❖

No sacred fire to bear witness for this wedding. Instead, there is the Sun and the Moon. A man, a woman and the secret spark burning between them.

No chanting of holy mantras, but just the symphony of their two beating hearts.

No seven vows on which to establish a future, but just this slow breathing, the emptying and the filling up of love.

No seven lifetimes, there is only the now: two garlands of pink lotus buds, with the freshness of the lake water still on them.

And yet, here, too, is the feeling of arriving.

❖

Home, the new bride realises within the hour, comes with a list of strictures.

Wash your hands and feet before starting on kitchen work. Pound the grain. Chop the greens finer. Cut the jackfruit into bite-sized pieces. *Not* the size of your bite but smaller. Grind the spices to a smooth paste. Churn the buttermilk to a froth. Season the dal. Stir the payesh: stir, stir, otherwise it will stick to the bottom and burn. Roll out the rotis faster. Lay the leaf plates and cups in a straight row. Remember to serve the eldest first. Use your right hand only. Keep to the correct order of dishes. Don't forget to ask if anyone wants a second helping. *Stop* smelling everything. No, you cannot stick your fingers into the food. No, you cannot eat till everyone else has finished eating and you have removed their plates. Scour the cooking pots clean. Place them right. You will have to be more brisk in the kitchen, Daughter-in-law. Knowing how to cook and feed properly is a woman's way of ensuring her family's survival. Come, now. Serve me first, then sit down and serve yourself. Yes, we follow this routine *every* day. Don't be disheartened. I will teach you. It's simple, really. All you have to do is be obedient and learn to anticipate the wishes of everyone. That is the key.

The hands that have expertly strangled and disjointed wild animals, skinned their bodies and scooped out their slime-covered entrails learn kitchen etiquette. To knead, chop, season, mix, shape and serve. Studying her palms a few hours later, she wonders if they are any longer her hands or do they belong to someone else? Though the melange of flavours lingering on her tongue are as enticing as the comfort of a full stomach, she gets the uncomfortable feeling that the kitchen and its weird rules are meant to carve, reshape and tame her just as surely as the neat stockade around the house controls the patch of land within from running wild. Is this what marriage is in their world?

10

The Runaway Hours

Alone at last with each other, wearing only the threads of their desire, they recognise that this is no longer another sequel of a night-time fantasy but a different nearness—for which a new vocabulary is required. Beyond the falseness of words, the unasked questions and all those barriers that give birth to differences, what works is touch.

He knows that he is attractive to women. Beneath the strongman image, they sense a warmth and sensitivity that make physical intimacy genuine and pleasurable. Frank desire had ruled his earlier encounters too, but never had any one of those been so complicated as this: pity had not diluted his lust, nor had self-disgust stained it. These feelings are new to him and they push out the finesse he might have ordinarily displayed in making the first approach. Also, non-compliance, a tiresome attitude that he has developed when around her, holds him back. At first—like two left feet trying out new dance steps—it trips them up.

Indifferent to his indifference, she has no qualms about being the wooer. Pushing him down, she twines her strong, willowy frame around him as smoothly as if she were his new skin, draws the curtain of her long dark hair over them and smiles at him, places his right hand on the curve of her hip and the left one on the swell of her breast. Her lack of coyness both repels and excites him. She reaches for his face, brings it closer. Her smell, musk, lips, saffron. The tip of her tongue wet and warm as a spring rain, probing—till his mouth, involuntarily, parts. Breathing him in, tasting his skin inch by inch, she moves down his chest. She presses her ear down to listen to his heart, its simple language—steady, insistent, flooding. Where is he not? He is on her tongue, in her nose and ears, in the deepest layers of her skin where pain and pleasure eat away at each other till nothing of either remains.

Initially, he feels the swirling currents of her passion with a certain self-satisfaction. Despite himself, his body takes over. A tide crests, too, in his veins. He pulls her abruptly into an embrace as cruel as wrestlers in a fight, a grip that seeks to punish. Skin burns skin. A bite for a bite. New wounds spring up in an outburst of tiny fires. Their bodies—don't ask where one begins and the other ends—interweaving into a single form they recognise as each other and themselves.

❖

Time loses its sanity. Ordinary lovers everywhere wait for nightfall, but these two live for sunrise, for those fresh, new-smelling, untamed intervals when they can steal away to dance their mad dances, drink their wine, sing up their love. The light alters for them, growing patches of murkiness to cover their capers. The hours become the crumpled sheets on which they come alive—while deadening themselves to the falseness of their marriage.

When dreams come true, they become reality, but this is not that. No prospect here of greying together. No yellowing of romance, no memories turning into dust, no waning of desire. Is theirs a real love story? Hard even for them to say. There is no tragedy waiting to unfold, no catastrophe lurking at the next bend. No one is about to die in it. No poetry. No justice.

Call it an encounter, dangerous, but the deliciousness of the illicit! Or more prosaically, an interval, a pause in the real action. Perhaps, it's best to keep it nameless: what happens in the forest stays in the forest. Like a void, it has a beginning and a middle but leads nowhere. What they cherish is in a free fall: you are my body, you are my soul, my blindness, my light. All that is perishable, all that is eternal. They find new ways to make their delinquency magnificent.

Borders mean nothing to her. She is fluid about who she can be: a she-wolf, a fish, a peahen. Air is her ruling element, her extended kingdom. Lifting him as easily as the breeze raises a feather, she takes him on a round of the world to places unseen by any human before. Seated on puffs of clouds, riding the cool, moist winds, they go to divine gold-tinted cities where the palace domes disappear into the blue and the walls are studded with a mosaic made of gems. Peaks hazy with fog, the breasts of hillsides, deep secret valleys, shorelines kissed by warm waves are their marriage bed; moss and sand, their pillows; water and sun-dappled shadows, their coverlets. They throw themselves at each other in quiet bamboo groves, fragrant mango orchards and elegant pleasure gardens, in sacred woods and colonnaded underwater mansions where silver-scaled fish tickle their feet. In brimming lotus pools and tumbling sprays that give off a seven-coloured mist; in dark caverns and narrow rocky clefts with no end in sight, they find and lose each other.

Grip and let go.

Again and again and again.

❖

They are sitting, sated, on a mountaintop. The sky, a pale eggshell blue is the perfect canvas for a sprinkling of pink-tinged clouds. On the gilded horizon, bold crimson banners are all that remain of the sunset.

'When it's time, that's how I'd like to leave you,' she murmurs. 'With a radiance of memories. You will remember, won't you?'

The breeze pushes his hair back. It makes him look youthful, without a care. 'How do I know that you *won't* return in some other form to haunt me?'

'Don't flatter yourself. Besides, shape-shifting is a deception. Is that cloud a lion's head or a forest fire? Was that leaf that fell on you earlier today a moth? We are all deceivers. Are *you* dead, as the world believes, or are you alive?' She sends him a teasing smile and lowers her voice to a whisper, 'Are *we* husband and wife?'

'You had better answer that yourself. Between the two of us, *you* are the trickster.'

Tilting her head to one side, she says, 'If you say so, but my tricks are simple ones. Cajole trees to bear fruit, make rain fall, grow back a stag's broken antler… these are possibilities. But I have an idea worth trying.'

'What?'

'What if I transformed you permanently into a different kind of animal? What do you think of that? We could become a *pair*—of rabbits, swans, wolves or owls. A sustainable living.' She sends him a coquettish look.

He shakes his head slowly. 'It's not for us.'

'Why not?'

'We are incidental lovers,' he says, gentle but firm. Impenetrable.

Her face becomes small, as if she is reluctantly surrendering a secret hope. *Why are you always so suspicious? I am not an illusion: neither my passion nor my love.* Recovering, she says in a casual tone, 'Incidental or accidental, isn't it the same? The waiting, the wanting. It eats up the hours we are apart. Such a waste of time. I wait for dawn so that my eyes can fill up with the sight of you again.'

'Don't belittle those hours of darkness. Think of it as sustainable loving. You are most visible to me when you are not seen.'

Her eyes spark in amusement. 'Liar or a poet, which one are you?'

'It doesn't matter which. Besides, my tongue isn't smooth enough for either. I can never be anything other than a straight-shooting kshatriya.'

'Yet, here we are, miraculously perhaps, in a marriage. A straight kshatriya and a crooked rakshasi. Husband and wife.'

He shakes his head dismissively. 'But I will change back to being what I really am. The world presumes that I'm dead, but that belief is wrong. When the time is right, I will be resurrected as myself. Bheemasen, the second Pandava Kaunteya.'

An icicle of fear pierces her heart. 'And after that?' she asks. 'What about us?'

His face is deadpan. '*What* about us?'

She looks at him mutely. *I can't lose you.*

After a moment, he sighs. 'You are seeking from me the kind of commitment I cannot give you. We—this relationship—my mother and elder brother insisted on calling it *a marriage* because they...' He stops abruptly. 'Never mind...maybe we should just call it an innovation, a new way of doing things.'

'I don't care what they call it, as long as you agree that it means the same thing to you that it does to me.'

He is silent.

The horizon fades into a purple mist. Shadows lengthen across the indigo valleys below. In the homes, lamps are lit and cattle locked in for the night. A chill wind picks up, shrieking as it rushes past their perch, as if it intends to mow down the deodars on the slopes and blow away the grey slate tiles off the roofs. A giant cumulonimbus grows into the sky, a multi-storeyed creation towering over them. Ominous as an arsenal. Silvery white rivers of lightning branch out of it, sizzling and crackling across the dark expanse.

She sees it a split second before she feels the jolt of

the explosion. The mountain trembles. There is a strong smell of burning in her nose. She knows instinctively that Indra, the Rain God, with his passion for creating weapons of mass destruction, is at it again. He has ordered the creation of a mighty astra.

But this time his forge is her womb.

11

The Unborn

Who is he?

He is No-Time. Never having known embodiment his is not a rebirth. Pristine, he brings no karma or predilections of his own. No feelings of déjà vu.

What does he look like?

The waters that keep him in suspension are unlit. Being newly incarnated, he curls into himself, as though still indistinct from the unchanging expanse within, containing only its calmness, its myriad possibilities. For a long time, he stays this way: serene, enlightened, not yet open to elucidation. However, something *is* changing; he is no longer timelessness but a new manifestation, shaped from this earth and its feral energies. Like all terrestrial life, he too is a provisional creation, subject to Time. He will become a story. This is its beginning.

Once upon a time.

There is only sound, the dull but steady echo resounding as if from a tale more ancient than this one. White noise—a continual bubbling, gushing and whooshing of life fluids—encloses him. Together with the periodic gentle rocking from his mother's movements, it lulls him to sleep.

He grows. The fires of life rage in him. They pulse in his cells, dividing, reshaping, aligning and assembling the anomaly that he will become. The spawn of a demigod and a rakshasi. A cross, or given the complex conflicting multiplicities zigzagging in him—deva, asura, naga, gandharva, rakshasa—a criss-cross. A riddle. On the ceiling and walls of his dim pre-natal chamber, fate is soldering his life to a grander purpose. Who will he be—a man, a monster or a superman? All three? Or is this existence a forgery?

Whose vanity knits him? Whose expectation and whose reality? Whose pride, whose downfall? Whose strength, whose shame? Whose myth, whose history and whose doom? Whose resolve and whose ambiguity? Whose head and whose body? Whose heart, hate, passion, fury? Whose fear, whose hunger? Whose love? Whose blood gives him his name? Whose puppet is he? Whose worm and whose god?

Having no inkling yet of the contraries that underpin his conception, the *why* of his creation will delude him.

Meanwhile, the clay from which he is being fashioned carries the template for its own continuation. Out of habit, buds open up in different parts. Ears, eye slits, a nose, limbs, fingers and toes, eyelids and fleshy lips. The shape of a hominid appears. Very quickly he grows. Moves his limbs and slowly turns his head this side and that, up and down, curls his toes, rolls up his fist. His mouth opens and closes. Finger and toenails sprout. But no hair. Not a single strand shoots out of his bluish-grey skin. Hair is power. One day, he will look at his reflection and wonder about his abject hairlessness. *What beast am I? Whose sacrificial victim?*

Ensconced in the undulating darkness, he continues to nap, but now the sleep is interspersed with longer hours of wakefulness. Endowed with extraordinarily powerful senses, he is aware that beyond his own existence there are worlds—to which he is connected. His mother's body is the terrain he maps first, from the physical processes that tie her to nature. These days, she is constantly hungry. The contents of her stomach create an interesting potpourri of odours. Dead ants are her first, feverish craving; they smell bitter and oily. Assorted meat stew: gamy. Smoked water chestnuts and mildly charred venison make his mouth drool. He loves the coolness of minty flavours in the leaves she chews to curb morning sickness, but puckers his lips at the tartness of raw mango that she consumes by the bushel.

At dawn, when she bathes in the lake, and its waters breathe on her skin, they bring to him a richness of smells—algae, fish, rotting leaves, wet mud. The breeze in her hair is scented with wild flowers and the delicate watery green of the young grass upon which she lies. As she gazes at the sky, he follows the tumultuous thoughts swarming in her head. In the bamboo groves, surrounded by the sound of leaves, wrapped in the arms of her lover, he senses her peace and contentment. Cocooned between them, the man and the woman, he is aware of the sexual want in her that arouses her partner. He smells the man on her, the strong, clammy, warm scent of male desire and catches a whiff of an undernote: an ineffable gentle melancholy that lurks deep, below the sinew. Like the sensual fragrance of the musk inside the deer, he, too, will hold on to the memory of this elusive love and look for it all his life.

For now, he listens.

Silence. A void, a fullness. The incessant noise of nothing happening, a dead time, a missing page, a quiet rage. The singing of birds, the chuffing of tigers, the huffing of bears, the mating cries of swamp deer.

Slowly, the soundscape becomes clear. The vibrations acquire distinct qualities. The ripping noise of an arrow leaving a bow. A death cry. Voices: soft, loud, harmonious, discordant, clear, muffled, polite, rude, caring, cruel, cold. Near and far, expanding and contracting, distending and disintegrating, the different tenors suggest to him a world of toughened boundaries far more complex than the crude sutures that stitch him together.

Vrikodar/Bheem. His father. A special voice, deep and confident, that stirs up a delicious, toe-curling charge in him. A ringing laugh that floods him with joy. He senses his father leaning on him, unknowingly seeking solace from his pure, warm animal presence. He listens to the secret hollow ache in his father's heart, the anger blowing in through the gaps, the dark menacing threats to break teeth with bare fists, tear apart limbs, claw out innards and drink the blood—of enemies. Together with the energy billowing in him, the unborn has inherited from his male parent a deathly enmity, but he doesn't know it yet and wouldn't care if he did. These moments with his father are all that he will ever have.

His mother's voice? It is the throb in his veins. Like the primal sound that births the universe, it is the breath within his breath, the word for which *he* is the meaning. It is benediction, it is comfort. It is morning, noon and night. It is the light he wakes up to. As she sings the songs that her mother had long ago sung to her, it is the soothing pillow under his head. It is the moon on a moonless night, the holy fire that never burns out. It is all the beauty in this world. And the next.

12

Faultlines

A child. His own. *Theirs. His and hers.*

He runs his hand through his hair, sends her a beleaguered look.

'Say something!' she urges impatiently. 'What do you feel?'

Frozen, can't you see? How can I allow myself to feel?

'But you've only just told me!' he says. 'Give me a few moments to take it in…I am happy, of course—for you. And for Mother too. Does she know?'

After a moment, she says, drily, 'She knows.' To his questioning look, she replies, 'She guessed it. Women see these things. They see the signs early. And your mother, as we know, has perfect vision.'

'Signs?' He looks her up and down. 'I don't see anything different.'

'She saw me collecting ants' eggs.'

'Ants' eggs?'

'To make a chutney.'

'That doesn't mean anything,' he says cautiously. 'Your food habits are different from ours.'

She shakes her head. 'You wouldn't understand. This isn't about habit, it's about taste...I just *had* to eat it.'

'What did Mother say?'

Hidimbi shrugs. 'Asked a few questions, nodded her head.' She sends him a look he can't read. 'I'm more interested in what you have to say. Don't you have anything to tell or ask?'

'I don't quite know what,' his voice tapers off. 'This is the first time that something like this has happened, erm, I mean...how am I expected to react? How do *you* feel?'

'Hungry.'

'Ants' eggs again?'

'No. I want to eat a wild goat. Whole. Roasted. But first, its blood has to be completely drained.'

He looks shocked.

A ghost of a smile flits across her face. 'We smoke the blood and cut it into chunks. It's delicious. You should try it too.'

'No, thank you. You keep to your kind of food and I'll keep to mine.'

'Your mother said the same thing when I offered

her the chutney I'd made.' Her look says that she has more to tell.

'And?' he prompts, with a faint smile. 'What did you say?'

'Nothing,' she replies demurely. 'I only said that we will be equal when we all eat the same.' Catching his reproachful glance, she adds, 'I cook what you all eat, anyway. Look at these burns on my hand. From making a mountain of rotis for you alone.'

He lifts her hands and kisses them one by one. 'We are equal,' he says, softly. A peace offering.

Shaking her head, she says, 'Not in love. I love you more than you love me.' The words come in a burst, as if it's a wisecrack, but she can no longer contain her heartache. Her face crumples. Tears rush to her eyes. She brushes them away angrily with the back of her hand. 'It's not what I thought it would be.'

Made uncomfortable by her emotions, he asks roughly, 'What did you think that it would be? Or were you blinded by what *you* wanted and did not see that I could offer you nothing except a few hours of passion. Even then, I married you...isn't that enough? What were you expecting from me? That I would remain with you forever? What did you hope for?'

'Heaven,' she sobs. 'But it's nothing like that.'

Drawing her into his arms, he rests his chin on

her head and mutters half to himself, 'If heaven is obliteration, it is.'

She tilts her head back and looks at him in astonishment. He meets her eyes. She blushes, ducks into his chest and mumbles against his skin. 'So, you admit that I do mean something to you.'

He gives a short laugh. 'I am made of flesh and blood too.'

She snuggles closer. 'I knew it! From the first moment…that *our* flesh and blood was meant to come together. *It has!* Vrikodar, *we* are creating a child together. Something new is beginning. Isn't it wonderful?'

He listens to her prattling on, but says nothing. After a while, she notices his silence and asks in a quieter voice, 'What is it, love?'

'Nothing,' he replies distantly. 'When will the baby be born?'

She wrinkles her nose. 'The baby! You mean *our baby*. Pick a name. Choose a name different from the usual rakshasa names. Or maybe Mata Kunti would like to pick one for her first grandchild.'

'A rakshasa name will be better,' he says brusquely. 'Since he will spend his life among rakshasas.'

She looks at him without speaking.

He avoids meeting her stare. After a few moments, he turns to her. There is a hard glint in his eyes. 'What

I meant was that his home is here. He will spend his life with his own people.'

'*You* are his father,' she says softly. 'You, too, are his own, aren't you? Isn't this forest where you live too?'

A frostiness enters his countenance. 'Home is not where you live,' he says evenly. 'It is where you belong.'

Her face goes blank with hurt. She looks away. It is dawn. They are on their favourite perch, the mountaintop. Skeins of wild geese thread the air around them. 'Look at them,' she says. 'Land, water, sky, there is no place where they cannot belong. The ability to adapt is innate in them, then why not in you? Isn't it a kind of independence—to choose for yourself and not have others choose for you? Isn't it what makes love different and beautiful? That it enables one to cross boundaries. It makes probable what was earlier considered impossible. That, too, takes courage, doesn't it? When I am with you, like right now, I experience myself, but I also experience you…I am not in the denseness of my desire alone, but in a clear, clean place of joy, sharing and utter contentment. Everything feels just right. It feels like a triumph…I want for nothing but to share my life with you, Vrikodar. However, I sense that, even after all the time we have spent together, though you *seem* happy enough with me, you don't feel the same way as I do. Why? Tell me what can I do to make you feel differently? Or should I simply change *you*? As I have said before…*I can.* We could become a pair of cranes, devoted solely to each other for life, and, like these birds, know no borders. The whole of creation would open up to us.'

He sends her a cautious look. Shaking his head slowly, he says, 'You can but you will not. Deep down you too understand the limits of enchantment. A beautiful illusion is what your magic can create, a desirable reality. But I have to *live* in a different one, an endurable reality. The truth that sustains the everyday world.'

'*Your* everyday world, Vrikodar. A world that never changes. I have lived among you people. You all are creatures of habit.'

'We live by conventions, yes.'

'And one of those is that you must not love a rakshasi. Hence your love for me cannot go beyond desire. Is dishonesty too one of your conventions?'

He chuckles. 'Ahh! You've seen through us. Some people have more trouble with their lies than others. Take Yudhisthir, who would rather pull out his tongue than utter a lie. But I am not like him. I am comfortable being the lie I am—clumsy as it is, it works for me.'

'You'd rather live in dishonesty than admit that what we share is special or meaningful. Do I mean *nothing* to you?'

He raises his arm as if shielding himself from a blow. 'How can you not mean anything?' he protests, laughingly. 'How many men, do you think, could lay claim to making love to a bloodthirsty rakshasi? That too takes courage.'

'Show-off!' She punches his shoulder lightly. 'But you don't fool me. The truth is that you want, *more* than anything else, to go back to your old life.'

The smile fades from his eyes. He looks away into the distance, his mouth drawn into a thin line.

How dejected he looks! After a while, she says softly, 'You are thinking, she doesn't understand. It's true. I don't understand you fully, but I want to know. What keeps you in Hastinapur? Why is it always on your mind?'

'How do you know what's on my mind?'

'Human thoughts are not difficult to grasp,' she says with a half-smile. 'It isn't my supernatural powers but marriage that has made me an adept face reader.'

He growls in mock anger. 'Stop stalking my thoughts.'

'Then answer my question: why do you still dream of returning to Hastinapur when there is nothing to keep you there?'

'*Still dream*?' He turns sharply to look at her. 'We are not dead...we *will* go back. It's not a dream.'

'But what will you go back to? You are dead to that world and it has moved on without you.'

'*No!*' He roars, as if she has touched a raw wound. 'You don't know the first thing about us.' He stops abruptly and clenches his fists.

'So…tell me.'

After a while, when he is sufficiently calm, he says, 'My parents left Hastinapur to live in Shatashringa. We brothers were born in the forest and spent our childhood there, but I can barely remember those times. We were dwarfed by the scale of nature around us: cloud-covered peaks, steep hillsides, narrow valleys, dangerous rivers, rain and mist. Our family was one more among the forest-dwellers. Like the trees that never moved, we too lived the same life from day to day, year to year. A simple, insignificant life. *However.*' His voice becomes more animated. 'However, all that changed once we came to Hastinapur. You know why? Because Hastinapur gave us a perspective. Our very first tour of the palace—just its kitchens—was an eye-opener for me. The size of the granaries, cowsheds, stables; the number of servants needed to maintain that level of prosperity. You cannot imagine the scale of it. Standing on the palace roof, we saw the city at our feet and beyond that, as far as the horizon lay, the Kuru lands. We had a clear vision of what we could become. During those years we spent living in the Kuru royal tradition, we grew to the proportions that were just right for us.' Seeing her bemused expression, he stops and looks about, distractedly muttering, 'How do I explain it to you?'

'I do understand,' she says softly.

'No, you don't. *You can't.* This forest has always been there, existed in exactly the same way since its beginning. But Hastinapur was designed by men. *Men of purpose.* It was a miracle formed by the vision of great rulers like Yayati, Puru, Dushyant, Bharat—their actions have shaped Aryavarta into the power that it is today. They set the norms on which long-lasting empires could be founded. They gave the Kuru empire the stability and the administration that is essential for richness to flow in, for everyone to prosper, for the weakest to survive. When we began to live in Hastinapur, we understood that we, too, are rooted in that tradition of empire-builders. The stream of life that flowed in our ancestors runs in us too. It is our birth right, our strength. Our dharma.'

She studies his face silently for a moment. 'Have you inherited only your ancestors' strengths and none of their weaknesses?'

He flounders for an answer. 'We have drawn our lessons from those too,' he says, finally, with a tinge of bitterness.

'What did you learn?'

'To rule is a sacred obligation. *One cannot just leave.*

However, my father did exactly that—left the kingdom in the care of his brother who quietly usurped it. Now, *his* sons believe that it is theirs. We will have to fight to get our kingdom back. That, too, is our obligation.'

'Are you going to fight your father's war, Vrikodar?'

'We owe it to him to fight.'

'And is it what you want from your son as well?'

'Obviously! Not only him, but *his* son too.'

'What if I say that *my* son will fight only if he, too, has a son's—a firstborn son's—right to inherit?'

'Impossible!' He stares at her, frowning. 'Is *that* what you have wanted all along?'

She shakes her head. 'I said *what if…*'

'It shows how delusional you are. Firstborn or not, your son cannot be an heir. This life that I am living with you is not my real life. That is elsewhere and neither you nor your son can have a place in it.'

'But this is *my* real life,' she says. 'You are in it and your unborn child as well. Look deep into my eyes and tell me that what we share is false. Whatever divides us has always been there, Vrikodar, but you and I have found a way to unite despite everything. We have found a way to be happy together. Isn't that a change from the years you spent in Hastinapur thinking that you belonged there, but found that you were in bitter competition with your cousins? This is a fresh beginning for us, but especially for you. Everything about this moment is new. Can't you see it in this soft glow of dawn? Stay with me. Why should we have only one son? We could create a whole world between us, a whole new world.'

A shudder runs through him. 'What an insane idea! Lust has made you crazy. The meaning of this world cannot be narrowed down to your body and my body or to our lying down together. If I were to live here with you forever, what would *I* be? *Your mate? Another rakshasa?* Do you know what that means? *I* would be destroyed by that life and you would be the cause.'

And I thought you were a god.

His words, like a furious storm, sweep away her dreams. The light in her eyes dims, but she continues to speak in a conciliatory tone. 'Instead of waiting for your elder brother to get a kingdom, you could be the king here. In your own territory, you would have the chance to grow into your true size, Vrikodar.'

His eyes narrow in suspicion. 'Are you trying to cause a rift between brothers?'

'But why would I do that?' she asks blankly. 'You spoke just now of your life before you went to Hastinapur. Were you not happy then? Families grow well when the seeds of love are sown in them through inclusion and cooperation, but there is something about the human heart that makes it more fertile for competition and the seeds of hate. In Hastinapur, with your arrival, perhaps those very seeds took root in your relatives. It led them to plan your death. You barely survived. Then how can returning to the same place, where your worst enemies live, be a good idea? How can you hope to be happy there?'

'This isn't about happiness,' he says. 'It is about who we choose to be, our self-respect.'

'You will restore your self-respect only by teaching your enemies a lesson, but will that not carry your enmity further? You are fighting to preserve your father's legacy, but isn't that also the legacy of violence? The world is big enough for everyone, Aryaputra. Isn't it better to pour your energy into building something worthwhile elsewhere for yourself?'

For a long moment, he looks at her with a contemptuous sneer. 'Don't preach to me, Rakshasi,' he says with a deliberate softness. 'What would you, who was born to live your life in this wild place, worrying only about your next meal or finding your next mate, understand about the vast and complex universe that I come from? *My* whole life is bound with that of my family. I believe that the throne of Hastinapur should come to my elder brother not by birthright alone, but because he is more deserving. *He*—not Duryodhan—will be a righteous king. Duryodhan, driven only by his jealousy of us, will repair the injustice Dhritarashtra imagines was done to him—a long time ago. Both father and son are trapped in the past, but Yudhisthir is forward thinking. He will act for the good of the world. However, virtue alone isn't good enough, it needs the backing of might to change things. Yudhisthir needs *me.* I cannot let what is convenient for me alone take precedence over the larger interest...But I don't expect *you* to understand this.'

Her face is pale. Bitterness closes her throat for a moment. She is trembling so hard that she has to tighten her fists to regain self-control. 'You think—*you think*—that just because this forest is my home, that I am wild too. A half-beast, am I? *You* can kill with the precision and ease you do because you believe you are not an animal. No animal could be as dangerous or unscrupulous as you. I saw you fight my brother, the rakshasa Hidimba. I witnessed how you killed him.'

'So what? He deserved that death! He wanted to murder us all...he was evil. I have seen the face of evil often enough to understand that it must be defeated.'

'You had your victory over evil, but did that make you its opposite—*good*? I saw how you broke his body and threw it away with utter callousness and contempt. Was that courage too or merely a crude display of your strength? He had a clan; when they came to prepare his body for a burial they wept at its horrible mutilation.'

He looks at her in astonishment. 'Are *you* trying to teach me the code of good conduct?'

She shakes her head slowly. 'I wouldn't dare, Pandava.' Her expression is sad, grieving. 'I am merely saying that the shadow of your imperfections has fallen on me too. When I first saw you, it was in a golden light and I was blinded. Since then I have seen you many times *in your true proportions.*'

'As long as you understand that they are far bigger than your desire.'

'I understand...Yes, I do understand that despite the experience of living in the forest, it is you who lack an understanding. Life is lived on very different terms here. It is not possible without teeth or claws. One has to use them every day merely to survive for one more day. This is different from your truth, your endurable reality, in that this *is* reality. The unchanging, *durable* reality. Ask any creature, even a simple beetle or an earthworm, what is most precious and the answer is the same: it is existence itself. Life. Every shred, every moment. The miracle of being is more precious than that of becoming. No matter who we are, all of us are caught in the same drudgery—of Time. But you believe that *you* are its master because you have mastered the art of killing. Your ancestors were men of purpose, you said. But they were men of violence too. Their empires were born from bloodshed. Was Hastinapur created out of nothing? Was nothing destroyed to build it? Will nothing be destroyed to get it back? The family of kings you come from has given you a sense of pride in your grand past, but was the complete picture ever revealed? Have babies not died, women not been enslaved, animals not been sacrificed, human settlements not razed to the ground, forests not been burnt down to establish the power of kings? And now, aren't *you* preparing to fight and kill your own kin? I cannot think of a single wild creature who would do what kings do or the scale on which they could do it. The allies, armies and arms you and your brothers constantly speak of, your plans to acquire them—what are they about? Your father is dead, but you with your dream of fighting to get his kingdom back are *choosing* to live the doomed life.'

'Not true,' he says. 'We are taking control of our destiny. We are putting all of our energies into lifting ourselves out of *this*—this senseless life. And we will triumph. *We will.*'

'The grandeur of your vision blinds you to everything else,' she says. 'You will cast me out of your life, but I love you and even if I wished it to, that will *not* change—whether you stay here or leave. However, I now see clearly how shallow your feelings are for me.

You cannot understand me in any way but at the level of the body. The hours that you spend with me give you pleasure but, after a while, they *are* pointless, aren't they? Then, what sense does it make for me to plead with you to stay? We are already moving away. You are driven, like the wind. But you want to go back and I forward. We are opposites. You want a war, death and destruction. But I want life—as it comes. Estrangement is our future. Well then, so be it.'

Shedding their skins, she without her glossy gossamer magic, he without his pride, they surrender to the future. They are adversaries, brought together briefly by fate. Their tragedy is that notwithstanding their separate destinies, they are also parents who will never be a family. *Us, we, our child.* These are love words, they allow a future to grow. But, to them all such words are absurd.

13

Birth

He is born on a clear winter night. A night when the sky is scattered with millions of stars and the light falls on the forest in ropes of silver. Close to dawn, the quiet explodes in an enormous cry that ripples through the ground like the tremors of an earthquake. Sweeping upwards, the sound surges over the trees like a mighty wind, increasing in chords and adding new frequencies that strip trees of their bark, tear the roofs off houses, send birds squawking and flapping into the sky, split hills and cause several streams to flow backwards and form subterranean lakes.

'That's a strong pair of lungs,' remarks the midwife. 'Let us pray that he doesn't use them to spray us all into oblivion.' She cuts the cord and takes the newborn behind a screen to clean him up before he is presented to his mother. Meanwhile, Hidimbi sits down, relieved that the long labour is over finally, and slowly sips a warm herbal decoction. After a few moments, she notices that the room is suddenly very quiet.

'Have you examined his teeth?' the midwife's daughter asks in a low voice. Youngest of the woman's nine children, the girl is her assistant at birthings. 'Does he have the full set of fangs?'

The midwife carefully pries the baby's mouth open and, checking the teeth, nods. Suddenly, he breathes out. Hot air singes her fingers slightly, sweeps through the room. 'A fire-breather!' says the midwife in surprise. 'I haven't seen one of those *ever*.'

'What do you mean?' Hidimbi asks turning towards the two women.

The midwife looks at her over the top of the screen. 'Was there a lioness among your ancestresses?'

'I'm not sure. You know how mixed up our genealogies are.'

'Still, I would say there are traces of a divine lineage in this boy.'

'What *do* you mean?'

'A god or a goddess. An ancient, powerful deity.'

'All rakshasas have supernatural powers,' Hidimbi says.

The midwife's daughter interrupts. 'But, they don't…' She stops mid-sentence and looks at her mother. '*Is* he a rakshasa?'

The midwife does not reply.

'What is it?' Hidimbi asks, feeling a rising panic. 'What is it that you both are not telling me? Does he have club feet, cleft palate, scaly skin or a forked tail?'

'*Those* could be passed off as rakshasa traits,' the midwife says. 'It's, erm…a bit unusual, but not to worry. Perhaps he will grow it after birth.' She sends Hidimbi a reassuring smile, but there is a hint of strain in it.

'What will he grow?'

Neither of them replies.

Hidimbi raises herself up slowly. 'Tell me! What's missing? Nose? Ears? Tongue? Or…?'

'Hair,' they both say simultaneously.

'No!' Hidimbi gasps, and sits down again quickly. 'Show me! Bring him to me.'

The midwife takes a few minutes to dry and wrap the infant in a soft cloth. Since his birth barely half an hour ago, he has started to grow and gain weight. In a few days he will be crawling, a week later taking his baby steps. This rapid growth is normal for a newborn rakshasa, as are the sturdy long limbs, the amber eyes and the pointed ear tips. But what is utterly unimaginable is his baldness. Hidimbi stares at the strangeness of him and is swamped with dismay. She looks up at the two women dazedly. *How could this happen?*

*Hair-**y**. Hairi-**est**.* These words had always portrayed rakshasas of every ilk. They applied especially to the males, who were blessed with the thickest manes in creation. Hair was everything to a rakshasa. His crowning glory, his vanity, his masculine pride. Among the rakshasas of the world there were annual hair parades with prizes for the best hair in different categories: Bushy, Furry, Curly, Shaggy, Longest Hair, Best Styled and so on. In such a hair-centred community tradition, a bald rakshasa, without even the basic thick, reddish-brown matted locks, was unacceptable—a monstrosity. A freak of nature. Though the mixing of bloodlines was known to produce creatures with strange features, such a one had, indeed, never been born before.

'Poor little fellow,' says the midwife's daughter with real pity. 'Is there a curse on him, I wonder?'

Her mother signals to her to be quiet, but Hidimbi is alarmed by her choice of words. *Poor. Little.* What could be more belittling to a rakshasa? Without dense, flourishing hair, he would be nothing. Zero.

The girl bites her tongue in remorse. 'Will oiling his scalp make a difference?' she asks her mother. She is trying to be helpful, but Hidimbi guesses that she can't wait to be the first to share this earth-shattering news with the entire forest. It cannot be kept secret.

The midwife, grasping for straws, immediately says, 'Oil? Why not? It has worked for other races who suffer from this problem, but if the condition is hereditary…' Her voice tapers off, leaving behind a wake of doubts and misgivings. Then, seeing Hidimbi's crestfallen face, she says in a more encouraging tone, 'We can certainly try some special hair oils.' Beneath the false confidence, Hidimbi's sharp ears catch the scepticism in her voice.

In that instant, a horrifying vision of the future unfolds before her eyes. She sees her son as the lonely young boy with no playmates, a child who would be pointed out and laughed at everywhere, a young man from whom all the nubile rakshasis would flee in disgust, a king who would command no respect and probably never rule. A hairless rakshasa is a powerless rakshasa and the sorriest creature in creation. This world was kind to no one, what would it do to her son? Pulling him deeper in her arms, she lowers her head to hide the tears that spring to her eyes. Hugging the babe protectively, she wonders: what am I going to do now? *How can I keep you safe?*

Seeing her misery, the midwife says quietly, 'You will have other babies, Hidimbi.' There is a finality in her tone that makes Hidimbi look up in alarm. The midwife's expression is one of concern, but behind that sympathetic gaze there is a grit that chills the new mother in Hidimbi to the bone. The midwife had helped bring many babies into the world, but how many had she eased out? 'You lose some, you keep some,' says the midwife in a soft, sad whisper, as if confirming Hidimbi's worst fears.

A loser? My son, a loser?

Her heart is breaking, but something unexpected happens that halts her despair in its tracks. The baby reaches out and grasps a lock of her hair, tugs at it and pulls out a handful. He looks at the strands in his fist, gives a triumphant gurgling laugh and kicks his legs furiously. Then he blows into his mother's face. This time, tiny flames emerge from his mouth. She feels a sudden, searing heat near her ear. There is the smell of skin burning. The babe opens his fist and releases the strands, they disperse around the room. After this little demonstration of his extraordinary powers, he looks at her and smiles. It is the sweetest smile in the whole world. Embedded in the pink stretch of his gums are the four pairs of fangs, glowing like the finest pearls, as if he is declaring to the world, of course, I am a rakshasa, who else would I be? She takes it as a good omen. *You will make your mark in the world. But you will do it by being different.*

'I've always had trouble getting the kitchen fire started,' she says to the two women watching her. 'That problem is now over.'

Though they are still a bit shaken, they smile in relief

at her little joke. 'It's nearly dawn,' says the midwife. 'We have to make the announcement soon about the birth. It is important to word it carefully. Shall I keep it simple? Queen Hidimbi has been blessed with a beautiful baby boy…' She stops as she catches her daughter staring at her aghast. The look on the girl's face says: *such a blatant lie, Mother?* 'Maybe we should just say *healthy,'* she quickly amends. 'He is clearly that. His birth weight is above average, but other measurements are normal. By the look of him, he is going to be a really big fellow… Have you thought of a name yet?'

Hidimbi, still dazed, shakes her head.

'He needs a name,' says the midwife firmly. 'A powerful one.'

'Since he announced his arrival with such a loud roar, we could call him Ravan the Second,' suggests her daughter, beaming as if she has found the perfect solution.

'My son is second to no one,' says Hidimbi.

'With a bit of voice training, he could be even more powerful than the first,' suggests the midwife.

'It's still a no.'

'Fire-breather?' says the daughter.

'He must have a name that *he* alone can own,' Hidimbi says. 'We have to create one especially for him.'

'Like what?' asks the midwife. 'Give us a clue.'

'It must be something that describes the uniqueness of him.'

'Egghead? Bighead? Skinhead?' rattles off the daughter, with the air of someone throwing all caution to the winds.

'No!' The midwife and Hidimbi yell together.

'Baldy, then?' The girl grins. 'It's certainly unique for a rakshasa.'

The midwife twists her ear and hisses, 'Don't be impertinent. Hidimbi is our queen, don't forget.'

'Think harder,' Hidimbi encourages her. 'Come on, give me some original names.'

The daughter looks at the babe's face intently. 'Hairless won't do,' she says, being more careful now. 'What about Perfect Circle?'

The midwife reaches out and touches the top of the smooth skull. 'Like a large clay pot.'

The daughter opens her eyes wide and then closes them. 'Hmm...pot, clay pot—what does it suggest?'

'Wealth, abundance, completeness,' chimes in her mother.

But it also suggests a vacuum, nonexistence, nothingness, thinks Hidimbi, dismally.

They both look at her in delight and say in one voice, 'Pothead!'

'We should make it even more individual,' Hidimbi says. 'Bald-as-a-pot. Ghatotkach.'

The mother and daughter pair try the newly created name on their tongues a few times in different tones, passing it to each other as if it were a game. GHATotkach. GhaTOTkach. GhatotKACH. GHATOTKACH.

'It sounds fine,' concedes the midwife. 'It has a royal touch. And, by suggesting abundance, it turns a loss into a benefit…But, what if someone somewhere discovers a miracle cure for this, erm, condition, and he grows hair?'

'He will have to change his name then,' Hidimbi says. 'On the other hand, with a name like Ghatotkach he could well be the innovator of a new style.'

'That'll be the day,' mutters the midwife, below her breath.

The first rays of sunshine are entering the birthing room. Cradled in his mother's arms, asleep, the infant is bathed in its golden light. At that moment he looks so tranquil that he could be mistaken for a heralder of peace from heaven. His head shines like a polished shield. He is every inch a noble prince.

❖

A messenger took the news to Mata Kunti. She, in turn, sent her blessings and congratulations to the rakshasa queen. But there was no word from Vrikodar though nearly a month had passed since his son's birth.

After the exchange on the mountaintop, Vrikodar and Hidimbi had continued with their daily trysts, but they never discussed the future. Hidimbi stayed on for a few weeks more with the Pandavas. However, when Kunti suggested that as the pregnancy progressed, she would be more comfortable with her own people, she seized the chance to get away and returned to the shala grove to await the birth. It would make the eventual parting of ways easy, she thought. But love doesn't like tidy endings. Somewhere in her heart, she longed to see Vrikodar, to be alone with him, to show his son off to him.

'A son *should* know his father,' says Vichitra. 'The Pandavas are about to leave in a few days, I'm told. Take Ghatotkach to meet them. It's the right time because he, too, is now grown up enough to remember.'

'He still hasn't spoken a word,' Hidimbi says worriedly. 'He eats, walks, runs, swings from trees with the monkeys. He is just like any normal rakshasa boy of his age. He has the full set of magical powers too. I saw him become a caterpillar yesterday, small-sized creatures fascinate him right now. Flies, beetles…'

'That's normal too,' says Vichitra. 'You loved turning into a glow-worm when you were his age.'

'But I can't help feeling nervous.'

'About *what*?'

'Will they, you know, be nice to him? I would not be able to bear it if they are cold and unkind. I don't want the first encounter with his father to be a bad one.'

'You've lived among them. Was anyone ever mean to you?'

Hidimbi chews a corner of her lower lip silently, thinking back to her time with the five brothers and their mother. Though everyone knew that the arrangement was temporary, she had tried to mix with them. But there was always a resistance: from within her as well as from the Pandavas. Just as they were imposters in the forest, she did not belong in their lives. Yet, no one had ever been unkind to her. In fact, they had all been scrupulously polite. Yudhisthir had maintained the same quiet, serious but considerate attitude that he had with everyone and Arjun the same self-assured air that she had first noticed about him. The Madreya twins had become quite friendly, often seeking her advice on the medicinal plants that could be used to cure sick animals. If there was anyone among the brothers who had treated her differently at all, it was Vrikodar. Alone with her, he had been a sensitive, passionate lover. In the presence of the others, he had acted, at best, as if he barely knew her, and, at worst, as if she was an irritant he had to put up with. This two-facedness of his had amused her at first and added a certain piquancy to the relationship.

But later she began to see it differently. He was letting her know where she stood with all of them: outside.

She replies to Vichitra's question. 'They were not mean to me, but…'

'*You* are his mother,' says Vichitra with exasperation. 'What others think does not matter as much as what you think. Are you ashamed of your son?'

I am not ashamed, but I am afraid.

❖

Kunti's first reaction is amazement. 'Is *he*…?'

Quietly enjoying the flabbergasted look on her face, Hidimbi smiles and introduces her son. 'Your first grandson, Mata. His name is Ghatotkach.'

Kunti stares at him, still dumbstruck. Giving her a moment to regain her powers of speech, Hidimbi nudges Ghatotkach. She prays that he will remember his first lesson, delivered a short while ago, in basic manners. 'Greet your grandmother,' she says. He dives with alacrity for Kunti's bare feet and gripping them, stretches out to his full length. His mouth is just millimetres away from her toes. Noting the speculative gleam in his eyes, Hidimbi yanks him up suddenly by the neck before he gives in to the temptation and scorches the digits to cinder.

'Please forgive me,' she says. 'He is still at that stage

when everything must be experienced via the mouth.' Kunti steps back quickly. But Ghatotkach returns to the supine posture and tilting his head upwards sends his mother an inquiring look. She understands. 'He's awaiting your blessings, Mother,' she reminds the older woman gently.

'What? Oh! Yes, yes…chiranjeev, chiranjeev,' Kunti stammers and gives an embarrassed laugh. 'My! How *big* he is.'

Hidimbi nods in agreement. 'He's growing well for his age, but a lot of him is baby fat. In a few months, when he is fully grown, he'll lose it.'

'Yes, yes,' Kunti says, nodding hard. 'I, too, had heard something similar, that rakshasas grow up differently, but it's still a—a surprise to see *how* fast. Just a few weeks old and already so tall and hefty. It's a marvel. Are you feeding him something to boost the growth?'

'Nothing special,' says Hidimbi. 'But he has a voracious appetite and prefers to cook his own food. He likes it well done.' She does not think it wise to elaborate any further.

Kunti smiles, as if in perfect understanding. 'Bheem, too, was like that, even as a toddler. Always curious about what was bubbling on the kitchen fire.'

Hidimbi nods calmly, though privately she is surprised

at the sharing of confidences from Kunti, who was never forthcoming about her earlier life. Thinking that this would be a good time in the affable mother-to-mother chat to ask the question that has been bothering her, she says casually, 'Do you notice anything else about him that resembles his father?'

Kunti looks at Ghatotkach appraisingly. 'He's going to be a mace wrestler,' she declares, with an air of authority. 'He has the shoulders.'

'What about the baldness?' Hidimbi asks, more pointedly. 'Any history of baldness in your family? Were any of his uncles born without hair?'

Kunti rounds her eyes in shock. 'No…*My* sons were all born with lovely silky hair. Even the two Madreyas had a lush growth as babies.' After a moment she says, 'Seeing him, I assumed you had performed his tonsure ceremony recently…haven't you?'

It's Hidimbi's turn to stare. 'You mean there is a ritual like that?' she asks, scandalized. 'We certainly don't have any such custom.'

'*No* first haircut?'

'No!'

'Well, then…' After a few moments, Kunti says, as if dismissing the matter, 'You must bring him up according to *your* tradition…I am, of course, glad to see him. In fact, I had kept ready a small token in preparation for your visit. A few baby clothes, in bark cloth. But I'm afraid they are already several sizes too small for him.' She looks at Hidimbi apologetically. 'I wasn't expecting this...'

'Your blessings are enough, Mata,' Hidimbi says. 'A bark cloth covering even in his size wouldn't last long. As he is a rakshasa the traditional dress for him is animal hide. It's more durable and also acts as a partial camouflage. I got the tiger skin ready for him just this morning so that he could wear it to visit you.'

Kunti looks over Ghatotkach again, taking in the bone jewellery, the two-horned headdress that he had insisted on wearing for this meeting. 'He is rather unusual,' she says in a dubious voice. 'But he's very respectful.' Aware that he is still prostrate at her feet, she says in a more benevolent way, 'You may get up, child.'

Ghatotkach rises, carefully dusts off the mud from his new tiger skin—of which he's rather proud—and looks up. He flashes a friendly grin at his grandmother. At the sight of the gleaming sharp-pointed fangs, Kunti's face blanches. 'Can he speak?' she asks.

'Not yet.'

'Oh!' She looks at him sceptically. '*Will he?*'

'He will speak when he is ready.'

'Hmm. I suppose.'

'I would like Vrikodar to meet his son,' says Hidimbi. 'Is he not here?'

'He has gone with his brothers to meet Rishi Shalihotra. They may take a while to return.'

'So, it's true, then…You are leaving.'

A cautious look and a brief nod from Kunti. 'As we had agreed.'

'I have not forgotten our agreement, Mata. I just wonder, is it safe for all of you to venture out into the world again?'

'It's safer than it was a year ago. The first anniversary of the burning is over.'

'Winter is coming to an end, but it's still very cold,' points out Hidimbi. 'Why not wait a few weeks till spring?'

'We cannot linger.' Kunti's voice is brusque. 'My sons are wasting their lives here.'

All at once Hidimbi comprehends why they are leaving in such a hurry: Kunti is afraid that her middle son may form an attachment to *his* son. Had they started planning their departure as soon as they had heard of Ghatotkach's birth? For some reason, this thought causes her to feel hurt. *I have spent so many days in her company. We got on reasonably well. Has she developed no sympathy for me? And what about her grandson—does her own blood mean nothing too?*

As if she had read her thoughts, Kunti clears her throat. 'You have been good to us, Hidimbi,' she says in a milder voice. 'I am grateful for everything. I mean it.' Her eyes are sincere. *I want you to believe it.* She continues, 'Ghatotkach is a beautiful, healthy child. After your brother's death you were alone, but now your son will be there for you.' She makes a significant pause.

Hidimbi looks at her blankly. *Am I expected to be grateful?*

After a moment or two, Kunti says, 'I know you will bring him up well, according to your custom. I'm not saying that I want him to become like us, but just understand that you married my son and we too are a part of your son's identity. Don't bring him up to hate us.'

Don't divide his loyalty to us. Hidimbi is silent, trying to fathom, as she had so many times before, what made the other woman tick. She feels no closer to the answer, but on this occasion, she senses that Kunti is lowering her guard, just a little. She is allowing Hidimbi to see who she really is. What would you do if you were in *my* place? she seems to be asking. The question hangs between them, its weight pinning them both down. One by one the answers rise and fall, all stillborn.

I am no one to judge her, thinks Hidimbi. From throwaway remarks and whatever Vrikodar had shared, she had learned a bit about Kunti's life and its hardships, but she had not lived that life from the inside. Even so, Hidimbi senses that Kunti is engaged in a long-drawn complicated battle. Her struggle is not just about the raw concerns of day-to-day living—her family's homelessness, the threat to their lives, the uncertainty of what tomorrow would bring—even though these alone are difficult enough for any human to bear. It is about keeping her sons together against all these odds; it is ensuring that each one of them survives and thrives. It is a journey that will end only when they have a kingdom of their own. Why is it so important for you to direct your sons' journeys? Hidimbi wants to ask. They are all grown men…aren't they old enough to determine how they want to lead their lives? But, of course, she does not. She doesn't think she will get an honest answer. Perhaps, there isn't one. Perhaps, despite her best intentions, Kunti is incapable of delivering one, or despite *her* best intentions, Hidimbi is incapable of grasping the fragility of a people who dream of greatness and the difficulty of the choices they are required to make to attain it. She only knows that while she has learned to respect this woman, she can never trust her.

Suddenly, she feels a strong urge to leave with Ghatotkach, to put as much gap between *them* and her son as she can. She looks around, but he is nowhere in sight, though there is a particularly loud bumble bee buzzing nearby. She wonders what excuse she can give as a reason for their sudden departure, but it is already too late. The Pandavas have returned from Shalihotra's ashram. Their voices can be heard through the trees. As they come closer, Hidimbi is surprised to see that they have discarded their forest attire of bark cloth and are now dressed in pristine white—like brahmins. Another disguise? Where are they headed this time?

They spot her. Joy leaps into Vrikodar's eyes. He stands stock still. There is an awkward silence among the others, as if something has suddenly fallen to the ground and broken into small, pointed shards that would require careful stepping over. Yudhisthir is the first to recover, responding with a calm cordiality to Hidimbi's greeting. One by one, she greets the other brothers, all except Vrikodar. Finally, she looks directly at him.

'I want you to meet someone,' she says with a casual familiarity, and calls out her son's name. He appears at once, like a genie, head bowed, hands joined in a namaskara. Without her pointing out who among the five is his father, he touches Bheem's feet.

Hidimbi wonders: how did you know?

A father seeing his son for the first time. Something as ordinary as this must happen every day. And yet every time it happens, it is a new beginning. It is also continuity, succession, the name taken forward. It is what every man dreams of. In the past months, it is what he too had dreamed, as well as dreaded. A bitter shadow-play of joy, trepidation and sorrow passes over Bheem's face. Hidimbi had steeled herself for this meeting, against the non-acceptance. But his face tells her something different: no, his son is not grotesque. He is not a freak. He is not evil personified. He is, to Vrikodar, quite simply, *his* son.

She sees the father bend down to lift the boy, his pleasure duly restrained because the others are watching. He kisses the top of Ghatotkach's head. He hugs him tight as if he couldn't bear to let go. She watches with surprise, as Ghatotkach turns to whisper something into his ear. His first words. Has he been saving them especially for Vrikodar? Vrikodar listens with deep concentration, stares into his son's eyes and smiles. Then he gently releases Ghatotkach.

Hidimbi is relieved but also troubled: *Vrikodar and I*...What were we when we started out but a man and a woman who wanted each other? What did we have to become? A husband and a wife—in an insufficient marriage. There was laughter and talk between us, but there was no shared image of the future. Whatever we desired, did it exist? Was it true? Did I get for myself the happiness I sought? *Did you*?

Yes, says his parting look to her. Despite all the

imperfections, its radiance is still with us. And the future is here too. I see you as the mother of my child. I am a proud father, unafraid. My son will be different. He will be a hero like no other. I recognise this strength that you have given me.

In return for nothing. It is not easy to love someone who cannot love you back. It happened to my mother and it happened to me. Mother and daughter, we were both unlucky, but I was perhaps luckier: everything that happened was with my consent. Once you come to terms with it, an unrequited relationship is the most beautiful feeling.

I am ready to let you go. Then I too am free to be myself. You will go back to your old life, but I am ready to find myself a new one.

❖

When they are back home among the shala trees, with Ghatotkach chattering nineteen to the dozen, Hidimbi draws him close and asks, 'What did you whisper in your father's ear?'

He looks at her without answering. His expression is strangely secretive. At that instant he looks like a different being, one who has suddenly, mysteriously thrown open a window and is asking her if she is ready to look at an unfamiliar sky. It is a look that she has never seen before on any human—the look of a mortal regarding the prospect of certain death because it is what gives him a purpose. As if the vision is too much for his comprehension, a shadow passes over his face. She sees the confusion cloud his eyes. *Who am I, Mother?* Then his gaze becomes lucid again, he repeats in a quiet voice the words of the pledge he had made to his father: call my name and I will come.

And dread finds its nest in her heart. *The man who fathered this child will never be a father to him. This child was born of my dream, my desire, my self-indulgence. He is the child of my imagination. I cannot bear to lose him.*

Grief isn't pretty or tidy. It feels like abuse, but it isn't. It feels like death, but it isn't. You can prepare for death, but no matter how early or clearly you foresee it, grief always blindsides you. The loss she has known is nothing compared to the bereavement she will know. She wonders: what good will I be to my son unless I can keep him safe?

Can she help him escape his destiny? Deep down, she knows.

14

Ghatotkach

Rakshasa education was simple, rooted in the timelessness of the forest and in the cycles that keep it alive. Birth, death, a new birth were all part of one long continuous landscape with no hiatuses. Beyond teaching their progeny certain skills essential for survival in the natural environment and for the defence of that environment, the average rakshasa parents left little by way of a legacy to uphold. Uncultivated they were, but not helpless or guileless. The forest was an unforgiving world, but it was known to them. They would survive so long as it survived. Cut off from them, it too would die. This is what Hidimbi has taught her son, in the hope that he too will see the forest as the place best for him.

Even so, news from the outside world reaches her. She hears of Bakasur's death at the hands of a brahmin from Ekachakra. The killer was one of a family of five brothers. Bakasur's relatives are livid. They and other rakshasas come to see Hidimbi.

'Tell us about the intruder who killed your brother Hidimba,' says Kirmira. 'We suspect that the same person killed Baka too.'

'It was too dark,' she says. It's clear from their faces that they don't believe her. As though a little ashamed, she adds, 'I fled.'

Their expressions soften in sympathy. She is aware that there is a rumour doing the rounds that she was abducted and raped by her brother's killer. It has generated anger and concern for her among the rakshasas. 'We have heard that Hidimba's body was badly mutilated. The way Baka's body too was left disjointed suggests that it was a ritual killing,' Alambusha says. 'This is someone with a black hatred for rakshasas. He is still out there, on the prowl. A serial killer of rakshasas is a powerful and dangerous creature. We must join forces against him. You too should be careful, Hidimbi. We don't want you to get hurt.'

'I promise to take care,' she says solemnly. 'Are you quite sure the killer was a brahmin?'

'A brahmin with the strength of a rakshasa.'

'Where are the five brothers now?'

'They have disappeared into thin air. Let's hope they have left this land for good, but be on your guard.'

Sometime later, word reaches her that the Pandavas are alive. They had surfaced in Kampilya, a city in the kingdom of Panchala. Its king, Dhrupad, had invited all kshatriya rulers to an archery contest with his daughter Panchali as the reward. Arjun won the contest, but all five brothers married the princess—at their mother's behest.

Hidimbi gives Vichitra the news. The yakshi nods as if she understands everything. 'This princess must be quite a catch,' she says.

'What do you mean?' asks Hidimbi curiously. Deep inside, she is a bit jealous of Vrikodar's new wife.

'When a family of brothers owns nothing, anything one gets as a reward must be shared equally,' Vichitra says.

'But does it make everyone equally happy?' Hidimbi cocks an eyebrow. 'Vrikodar's appetite at mealtime was far bigger than those of his brothers. Mata Kunti always said that he had to be given more to eat.'

'We're talking of a different appetite,' Vichitra says with a puckish grin. 'But Mata Kunti will find a way, I'm sure.'

'What do you mean?'

'In this matter, an impartial distribution is one way of ensuring that no one is made to feel left out and everyone shares in the family's good fortune. This marriage *has* brought them that…They now have the backing of powerful relatives.'

'Will they get their kingdom back?'

'Not unless their cousins give it away to them. Why would the sons of Dhritarashtra do that when they believe that it's theirs?'

'So…?'

'Wait and watch.'

❖

There is a spate of fires in the forest.

'Tell the little monkey of yours that this is not Lanka,' grumbles Vichitra. 'He doesn't need to scorch every rakshasa who makes a remark about his baldness.'

'He thinks they are ridiculing him!' Hidimbi says. 'They won't let him join their hairy gangs. It has turned out just as I had feared.'

'It's you who worry too much about the ridicule,' Vichitra scolds her. 'If you stopped doing that, he would probably stop harassing them and other people too.' She gives Hidimbi a stern look. 'Don't you see that he is going the Hidimba way? I have heard that he hates the brahmin priests who come to the forest to perform their rituals. Next, he'll be grilling them over their own sacred fires.'

'No, no, he won't go that far. He is just a bit angry.

Males of all ages are self-conscious about being hairless. It affects their self-confidence.'

'That's true, but tell him not to take these taunts personally. When people don't understand something because they've never encountered it before, they are suspicious and afraid.'

'But these are his own people! This forest is his home.'

Fixing Hidimbi with a hard look, Vichitra says, 'It's his prison too. He is restless, bored and lonely. It is not the same forest to him that it is to you. Ghatotkach is not *you*, Hidimbi. He was born different. He was meant to experience life differently from you.'

❖

Hidimbi cannot deny the truth of Vichitra's words. Ghatotkach is a constant source of worry for her. The delighted astonishment that characterized his early experience of the forest is gone. Its rhythms bore him. With every passing day, he finds it increasingly stifling. His loneliness finds an outlet in mindless destruction. He has become edgy and hot-tempered, a menace to the forest itself. To add to his discontent, the world outside is changing. It calls out to him. Hidimbi worries about the excessive interest he takes in the affairs of the Pandavas, keeping his ears open for every bit of news.

He rejoiced when they acquired their own kingdom,

Indraprastha; when his father Vrikodar killed the almighty Jarasandh, the tyrant ruler of Magadh, and when Yudhisthir announced that he would hold a Rajasuya yagna that would make *him* the most powerful of kings.

Hearing of the preparations for it, Ghatotkach goes to Hidimbi and says without any preamble, 'I want to go to Indraprastha, Mother.'

'You will not be welcome.'

'I disagree. My uncle Yudhisthir is a righteous king. They say that he has invited the Kauravas too.'

'Those people are his relatives.'

'I am his eldest nephew, Mother. The first-born grandson of King Pandu. Why would he not welcome *me*?'

'My answer is still a no.'

He is clearly disappointed, but he has come prepared to make her change her mind. 'This forest is a gilded cage, Mother, where you want to keep me safe. But the life you want me to live doesn't interest me. It isn't what I was born for. I want to spread my wings wider. I want to fly right up to the heavens.'

'It's the same sky everywhere, Son. Here and in Indraprastha. Unlike this earth, mortals don't own the sky.'

He sends her a crooked smile, knowing that it is

one of the ways to win her over. 'Let's just say then, that I'm curious, that's all.'

'Your curiosity is dangerous.'

'You always said that my father was restrained by his mother. Give me the independence that she did not give him.'

'You are already independent. You can change your form anytime: be a bird, see the world from above, be a fish and explore its gushing streams and rivers. You would not feel bored or lonely if you could just understand that you have the power to enjoy this earth in a way that ordinary humans cannot.'

'Don't talk in circles, Mother. You know very well what I mean. *Let me choose*.'

'I know what you will choose, Son. It's *they* who will not let you choose. They will trap you.'

'Trap me, Mother?' He laughs. 'I am a rakshasa. No one is stronger than me.'

'They are your blood. You have no defence against them.'

'As my blood, they are my people too. Why would I need a defence against them?'

'Because they don't see you as the same as them.'

After a moment's silence, he asks, 'Does that matter?'

'Yes...If you see them in their own world, you will be dazzled by its richness. You will begin to believe that *that* world is yours too. Their way of thinking will influence you. You will create the same ladder of desires by aspiring to obtain what they prize—chariots, weapons, a treasury filled with gold, lands, armies. Overpowered by your desires, you will become blind to the real riches which are yours right now. You will look down on all this plenitude, let it go to waste. But that is not the reason why I don't want you to go. You imagine Indraprastha to be the grandest city, but I see it becoming a graveyard. These are people who will fight amongst themselves.'

Ghatotkach grins. 'Rakshasas aren't exactly peace-loving, are they, Mother?'

'Our fights are not premeditated. Our hatred is open and lawless, it does not know how to feign. It is not sinister and scheming like theirs. Our fights do not lead to total obliteration as theirs do. You know how Indraprastha grew prosperous: by burning down an entire forest, by overpowering Magadh, by enriching its treasury with plunder.'

'I see it differently—Indraprastha prospered because of a grand vision and great effort. You should hear the stories about it. My uncle Yudhisthir has created a new and powerful empire. This forest is nothing in comparison to its size and influence. The rulers of other kingdoms pay tribute to him. Through vision, enterprise and industry, he has brought about a glorious age. I wonder what it must be like to live among them, to have that freedom to dream…Every single day that I live here is exactly the same as the one before and the one to come. Can't you understand that I want to be part of something that allows *me* to grow? I want to shape the world like the Pandavas are doing.'

His words give Hidimbi the sense that Time has come a full circle. She recalls the Pandavas' stay in the forest. Mata Kunti had called it a waste of time. Vrikodar had constantly dreamed of beating up his cousin Duryodhan. They had all lived daily with the dread of extinction, yet their dreams had remained grandiose.

'What will you do there?' she asks. 'What will you become?'

'I am a fighter, Mother. I will learn to be a better one. Their military schools are the best.'

'Those military schools are not for the likes of you. They train kshatriyas in warfare against each other. But all kshatriyas are united in their hatred of us rakshasas.'

'I am not the same as other rakshasas. I am *their* blood.'

'A half-blood,' Hidimbi says curtly. 'You will fight their wars, but when you are sacrificed, your death will not be a loss to them.' Seeing the hurt on his face, she pauses for a moment then adds in a gentler tone, 'It will matter only to me. *I* am afraid of the emptiness, if I were to lose you. It will exist only for me, and that is what frightens me the most. How can one being represent all of life? Ask me. I am a mother. You are my whole world.'

She has never spoken this frankly to him. He stares at her, stunned. It is a look of anger and confusion. 'Does my father *never* think of me? Is that why he has never come to see me or called for me? In my heart, I don't believe it…If I cannot find a place there with his people, then why do I feel caged *here*? To which world do I belong? Why do I feel like an outsider everywhere I go? What is the lie that I am telling myself? I am in a torment, Mother. A crude, uncivilized rakshasa or a brave fighter? *Who am I*?'

Years ago he had asked her that question. She had not known how to answer it, but now she can no longer look away: he is in utter despair.

I belong here, but you don't. You don't belong anywhere.

Life nourishes those who are open to it. From the instant we enter this world and draw our first breath, the world too is immersed in us. At that moment, desire fastens itself to the new life. While our bodies' needs allow us to live, it is something else that keeps us alive. It is the belief that there is beauty in this world. I beheld that beauty every day in the forest. I felt it in me when I was with your father. But, when you were born,

I held it in my arms, fed it with my breasts. In you, my son, I have seen something beyond myself. Just as every shala tree reaches towards the light, everyone needs a patch of sky. I cannot deny you the chance to gain yours. You will have to find your place in the world or make one for yourself, but how can you do that unless I let you go?

'All right,' she says aloud. 'You are free.'

He cannot believe his ears. 'Do you mean it?'

'Go wherever you want...I give you my blessings. I burned my bridges, Son. But I cannot stop you from building a new one, if that is what you really want. Build the bridge, but make sure that it is a strong one.'

❖

Over the years, he had come to see her. His stays were short, sometimes just a day or two, but they reassured her.

On one of his early visits, he told her that there were military schools in the south where boys as young as seven years and even girls from all backgrounds were admitted. It was to one such place that his uncle Yudhisthir sent him to train. His guru advised him that given his immense physical strength, he, like his father Bheem, should specialise in duel fighting.

'I like that, Mother,' he said. 'I understand it. When

two armies fight, the outcome is often mixed. But when two warriors fight, it's clear. You win or lose.'

Her eyes take in the change in him, she listens with mixed feelings. *He is happy.* His face shows it. His body too has changed: it has developed the agility, flexibility and the confidence that comes from an inner discipline. The taming of his brute strength and volatile nature has made him even more lethal. She'd heard that he was some sort of an icon for the younger generation of rakshasas who had formed a cohort of their own. He understood his power now and it had helped him in establishing a closer relationship with the Pandavas.

'The world isn't twofold anymore,' he says. 'Good and bad, them and us, upper and lower...These crude distinctions are fading.'

'To them you will always be a rakshasa.'

'A rakshasa,' he repeats with a grin. 'But also a trained fighter, an invaluable asset.'

She shakes her head, but says nothing.

❖

It was inevitable, she realises, when he comes to give her the news of the coming war. This is her last chance. She waits for the right opportunity to bring up what's uppermost in her mind, but something holds her back. Till he brings it up himself.

'I can see that you are worried for my safety,' he says. 'You never worried about it before. You *know* that there is no one stronger than me.'

'This war's roots lie in the family matters of the Kurus,' she says. 'When Yudhisthir gained his own kingdom and, subsequently, when Vrikodar killed Jarasandh, the Pandavas had their chance to build a great empire. But Yudhisthir himself gambled away everything and the Pandavas were exiled for thirteen years. You, my son, played no part in those events, hence this war has absolutely nothing to do with us. Stay away from it.'

'I cannot,' he says. 'I have been called.'

'Say no.'

'The world is shifting, Mother. It is becoming more complex.'

'*Their* world was never simple, but now it's a mess.'

'There is no *theirs* and *ours* for me. That divide doesn't exist in my head since I belong to both worlds.'

'If you think like that, you will have no choice but to go.'

He sticks out his chin slightly. 'I *choose* to go. And I am not alone. There are other kings too who had nothing to do with the dispute within the Kaurava clan, but they will be in the fight.'

'They are all kshatriyas. This war is going to

reorganise their society. Naturally, they will be asked to pick sides. When you have no vested interest like them, you should be neutral.'

'It isn't only self-interest that makes them choose which side to fight for. Many of them are related and they will fight for their kin.'

'It's still no concern of ours.'

'Mother,' he says with an unusual gentleness. 'Had you ever wanted my help, I would have come immediately, but you never did…My father and my uncles have had a harder time. They had to give up their kingdom. For twelve years they wandered from forest to forest, and in the thirteenth year, they lived as the servants of the king of Matsya. I have nothing but respect for them, they have endured their troubles with courage.'

'*And* with some aid from you,' she says tartly. Though she doesn't mean it as an accusation, that is how it sounds even to her ears.

'I only assisted them when they needed it—in the forest. Compassion is what *you* taught me, Mother. By allowing me to go into the world outside the forest, you freed me from the resentment I had against my father. When I helped them, I learned to see them as my own. Abhimanyu, my uncle Arjun's son, is like a brother to me. We are friends.'

Angry words rise to her lips, but she remembers suddenly how friendless he had felt in his childhood and remains silent.

'My father has called me because he needs my assistance. He has been the strong one among his brothers and they have always relied on him. But who can he rely on except me? I am his son. Who else but a son would redeem his father's honour?'

'Father's honour!' She gives a bitter laugh. 'You have started to talk like them too...But what about me, Son? Don't you owe me something? *I* am the one who will lose you.'

'I too will lose you, Mother,' he says in a quiet but careful voice, as if holding his emotions at bay. 'The thought makes me weak...but it is the fragility of love that makes it so precious. Do you think that I am not afraid of being killed? Every creature who lives in the forest has an instinct for survival. A rakshasa doesn't hesitate a second to inflict pain on another, but neither is he scared of pain...We do not lack physical courage. Yet we are despised because our strength is not seen as praiseworthy but as condemnable, a feature of our bloodthirsty, uncivilized character. However, the same violence in a kshatriya is lauded and celebrated...What better way is there to force them to recognize their hypocrisy towards us than to use our natural toughness towards a noble kshatriya cause? They say that this war is going to be fought for dharma. There are rules that both sides have agreed upon. I want to see for myself exactly how such a war is fought...My father had pledged in front of everyone that he would tear open Dushasan's chest and drink his blood. He will, undoubtedly, keep his vow, but will it make him more like me—a rakshasa? Or will he become a god? It is being said that the dead of Kurukshetra will all be equal, all heroes...There is a slim chance that I too may die on the battlefield, but that, to me, would be a worthwhile death. Having accepted the gift of a rakshasa's martyrdom, even *they* will be forced to recognise his courage. I am alone, as I always was, Mother, with only my shadow for a companion. But I, alone, am the son of Bheemasen and Hidimbi. The world knows that I am strong. I want it to know that I am lion-hearted too.'

Only Vrikodar's son would speak like this, she thinks. The same boldness, the same conceit...I will lose him too forever. Yet, despite her fears, she feels a flicker of pride.

'Go, Son, fight,' she says. 'There will be no defeat for you.'

15

Death Blow

He lies on the rim of the night, the blood seeping from the wounds he has received a while ago. Though his life energy is draining away, these injuries are pinpricks compared to the devastation from the final blow. When the missile punctured his chest, he didn't feel a thing. It was after a few minutes that he realised he had been downed by a weapon of unbelievable power. The damage was incalculable. What had it *not* destroyed? His lungs were on fire. Heart, liver, kidneys, bones had all been shredded in the few micro-seconds that it had taken the projectile to exit his body, leaving barely a small hole in his upper back. Yet, it was a slow, painful dying. His distress was made worse by the knowledge that his final task was unaccomplished. He had failed his side.

Kill Karna. Two words. Hearing the order, his chest

had swelled with pride. *I am the only one who can do it.* The moment had arrived when he would reveal his mettle to the world. He'd fought on other days too, in one-on-one combats against warriors whose determination and prowess matched his: Alambusha, who too was a rakshasa, Duryodhan, the Kaurava prince who was his father's deadliest enemy, and Bhagdatt, the king of Pragjyotish, who despite his old age turned out to be the most feisty of warriors. But these duels were mere appetizers to the one which he had been told to fight with Karna. It would be his toughest fight, but he'd looked forward to it, not merely to show off his strength, skill, cunning and experience against a formidable foe, but because the timing was entirely in his favour.

A battle after sunset had never been fought before. It was against the rules of engagement agreed upon by the leaders of the two armies. But, like other rules that had been broken, this one too was cast aside, at the end of the fourteenth day. While dismay and confusion filled the soldiers of both sides, he had been delighted. Darkness was his secret weapon. Past the border of twilight, a more primitive strength crested in him, the blood of strange creatures—saw-toothed, horned, humpbacked, of gigantic proportions, wild, snarling and cruel, ready to maim and mangle. By controlling their savage energies, he could conjure the most terrifying illusions.

All night, Karna had lorded it over the field, his arrows burning trails of destruction through the Pandavas' army. Their soldiers had started to flee. It was then that Krishna had sent for him. Taking him aside, he said: 'Hidimbiputra, you alone can save your friends and kinsmen from drowning. With your unique skills and valour, accomplish that which is worthy of you, your mother and your father. Be the raft in this battle that will save the sinking Pandavas. It is for this selfish reason that fathers desire sons: they are expected to rescue their fathers both in this world and the next. You, a rakshasa gifted with magical powers, boundless strength and great courage, are indestructible. You, Satyaki and Bheem are our three finest warriors. Satyaki will support you, but you must engage Karna all by yourself. Kill him.'

Elated by the responsibility he'd been chosen for, he'd made a promise. 'I will spare no one. Not the brave, not the cowards. Not even those who surrender and beg for mercy. Tonight, I will be a true rakshasa. I will follow *my* dharma.'

With bronze armour covering him, he rode into the battlefield on an eight-wheeled chariot drawn by strange elephant-like beasts. The vehicle was covered with bear skin, decorated with flags and packed with an arsenal of his best weapons. On the flagpole, high above, fluttered his special flag with the emblem of a vulture. 'Where is Karna?' he had roared, adding as a special effect a discharge of flames from his mouth.

'Face me first,' a voice replied. It was his old adversary—Alambusha.

'Gladly!'

Barely were the words out when Alambusha's flight of arrows pierced him. Goaded, he'd gone on a rampage like an elephant driven mad. He chopped Alambusha's charioteer to pieces, destroyed his weapons, broke his chariot and screaming in rage rained arrows on Karna, Alambusha, the Kaurava army. While the soldiers fled, Alambusha turned on him and punched his face. For a moment, he'd trembled on his feet. Then regaining his balance, he had struck back, pulverizing his adversary. Slashing Alambusha's head off, he'd lobbed it into Duryodhan's chariot. Devilry dancing in his eyes, he'd taunted, 'They say that anyone who respects dharma should never go before a king, a brahmin and a woman without a gift. Here's mine—your friend returned to you. Next, it's Karna's turn. Then yours.'

He had to give Karna his due. The man was unflustered. There was neither arrogance nor anger on his face, just the cool strength of someone who recognises and respects his opponent's power. It was, Ghatotkach admitted to himself, good to feel that his adversary regarded him as an equal. Each afflicted the other with well-matched blows, each weathered the onslaught with resilience. Arrows criss-crossed darts of fire. Wounded, they fought on, blood streaming down their bodies. He had used his magical powers to create terrifying images of snarling tigers, roaring lions, hissing serpents, iron-beaked vultures and monstrous rakshasa warriors descending on the battlefield from all sides. The mirages started a stampede among the armies. Crying, 'All is lost,' everyone had run away in fear. Only Karna remained. He had dispelled all of Ghatotkach's phantasms with his arrows. Angered and challenged further, Ghatotkach had raised a divine, thousand-spoked chakra and hurled it, but that too Karna shattered to bits. He had then flung his gold-plated mace which Karna destroyed in mid-flight. What next? Suddenly, Ghatotkach was everywhere, in a thousand horrifying forms all created by magic, a giant body cloned multiple times, hundreds of heads with glaring red eyes, teeth bared in a snarl, golden earrings blazing like twin suns dangling from his ears. Now big. Now thumb-sized. Now descending from the skies in a golden chariot, now rising in smoke clouds from the red-hot fissures that appeared in the earth. And always edging closer to his foe, till they were face to face. 'Sutaputra, I am going to wipe you out,' he had sneered, enjoying the moment and wishing to prolong the pleasure. Karna had looked back at him with a cool, almost indulgent, half smile.

He had invoked a deadly weapon and aimed it at Karna's chariot which had immediately disintegrated. But the charioteer's son had thrown up a thick cloud of arrows. Creating a gap in the shield, Ghatotkach had used his maya magic to generate a red cloud that shot bolts of lightning and rained meteors on the battlefield. Then came a shower of weapons, arrows feathered with gold, lances, axes, maces, gleaming swords, spinning chakras. A steady, unrelenting stream of weapons that pierced, sliced, chopped, smashed the armies indiscriminately. Chaos. A deafening din of a thousand war drums. Everywhere rose wails: Hai! Save us! Slaughtered animals, some still alive and screaming in pain. Headless warriors. Trapped warriors. Wounded warriors. Carnage everywhere, in every corner. In all this, unmoved, stood Karna, an island of calm.

Watching him, Ghatotkach wondered what was going on in his mind. That composure was deceptive and disconcerting. Never mind, he had a few more tricks up his sleeve. *Kill Karna.* The command echoed in his head.

❖

Strange how those scenes are playing back at this moment when everything else is falling away from him. *Why am I seeing them now? What did I miss earlier?* He is aware of the weird beauty of the battlefield bathed in blood, of the momentous fight he has just lost. Someone will surely live to tell this war's story, but will there be spectators who would narrate this epic duel? Will they know that he had recognised the precise moment when the game ended? Something had changed in his opponent, he sensed. Karna had come to a decision: closing his eyes, he'd held up his hand and the all-powerful dart had appeared. It had remained suspended in the air, as if it was not to be sullied by human hands. Sleek, lethal, glowing, Ghatotkach recognised it for what it was: the Vasavi Shakti, the spear that was Indra's gift to him. At the sight of it, a cold dread had gripped Ghatotkach. He had recognised a supernatural divya astra, a shakti, imbued with a magical power far greater than his own. He'd also understood instinctively why Karna had not used it earlier. It could be used just once. Something this special could only have been invented by Indra. Hence, its use had been preordained. Even if he turned and ran as fast as he could, he would not escape it. His time had run out. *This is it.* Nothing left to be done now but to salvage for himself a memorable end. An honourable death. He'd enlarged his body to the size of a mountain. Rising into the sky he watched the terrified humans below, frantically running for cover as a violent wind took hold of the battlefield and bolts of lightning began to pummel the earth, bathing the entire battlefield in brilliance. At that moment, looking straight up at him with an inscrutable expression, Karna had sent the missile speeding towards him. It passed through his body like a wave and disappeared into the clouds. Back to its inventor. He is falling now, a mountain crashing slowly. Debris now this body, vital organs ripped to ribbons, lungs ablaze, breath turned into smoke.

But even as he falls, he hears Krishna's voice say clearly, 'Make sure that you fall on the enemy.'

Done. An entire Kaurava akshauhini destroyed. His parting gift.

How quiet it is. Around him, like men enjoying a hard-earned rest, lie innumerable dead. Dawn is not far away. A rosy half-light bathes the blood-soaked earth in a melancholy splendour. This twilight was always his strength. His senses, though shutting down and leaving his body, are still capable of revival. *One last time, let me know this earth.* Suddenly, he is everywhere again, seeing all, hearing everything, eavesdropping even on the fading thoughts of his fellow men, the swirl of final images rising from their brains: home, field, village, river, father, mother, wife, child, sweetheart, friend. Regret. Relief. Love. The sky is cloudless and silent, the air cool. He feels its caress. *Mother, she knows. She had always known that this is what it would come to.* The other dead will be given their last rites. Will they leave him here on the battlefield for the vultures? A rakshasa who failed...He couldn't rise to the task he'd been entrusted with, but who had known what Karna had saved up? By the time the stories are circulated and his mother hears them, they may say something else. She will not believe it: to his mother he was always a winner. This disappointment is his own sad reckoning.

Karna, the hounded creature, lives. Ghatotkach, the hunter, dies.

From the Kaurava camp come sounds of celebration. On the other hand, in the Pandava camp there is an eerie silence. No one had foreseen his end. It has come to them as a terrible shock. They were his side. His task was to protect them. *Be the raft in this battle that will save the sinking Pandavas.* Krishna's words. What would he say now that Ghatotkach had crashed so spectacularly?

Through a swelling wave of pain, his spirit, still tied to his senses, is aware of everything. He sees them: his side. They are in a huddle of grief. Vrikodar, his father, has turned to stone. Yudhisthir, the uncle who never hid a special fondness for him, laments aloud. Arjun, Nakul, Sahadev look down and slowly shake their heads. And then, he sees Krishna join them. Here he is. Face wreathed in smiles, exuding an air of triumph. Slapping

Arjun on the back as if he were the champion, he says, 'Congratulations!'

They stare at him in silence.

'We have lost Ghatotkach, our finest warrior,' says Yudhisthir quietly. 'It is a time for grieving, Madhusudan. Your joy is untimely, unseemly.'

'Let me tell you why I'm so thrilled,' says Krishna. 'In plain words: Arjun has nothing to fear any more. That weapon used on Ghatotkach was, as you all saw, infallible. Karna had been saving it up for Arjun alone. Knowing that he had it with him, my entire focus was on somehow keeping Arjun out of his sight. But now that Karna has expended the shakti on Ghatotkach, he himself is...*as good as dead.*'

Bheem draws in his breath sharply. His nostrils flare. 'You knew it, didn't you? None of us knew that Karna possessed this lethal weapon...but you had known all along.'

Krishna's smile deepens. 'Drona decided that the fighting would continue into the night, not me. The Kauravas were under a strain after Arjun succeeded in hunting down the Saindhava king, Jayadrath, and killing him, just before sunset. My guess was that Duryodhan, who was no doubt devastated by the loss of a powerful warrior, would compel his commander-in-chief to do more to win. Drona took this call to fight despite knowing the rules.' He shrugs lightly. 'How could I pass up the chance to use Ghatotkach? His already phenomenal strength *grew* at night. The timing was a force multiplier for us. It made the rakshasa unstoppable. There was every chance that he would kill Karna, who, by the way, knew it too…Karna was fully aware that he was very close to dying last night…He knows what the loss of the Vasavi Shakti means to him personally. His golden armour gone, divine earrings gone, and now this infallible weapon too used up…Karna is a mortal now. Though still invincible, he can be killed. But only by Arjun. Arjun can *now*…kill him.' He looks at the grim faces around him. 'The rakshasas are all dead. Hidimba. Baka. Kirmira. *They all had to die.* A rakshasa is an enemy of dharma. Ghatotkach too. If Karna had not killed him, *I* would have had to do it.'

'An *enemy* of dharma?' Yudhisthir repeats, shaking his head. 'Really? He was Bheem's son, just as Abhimanyu was Arjun's son. Ghatotkach was *our* son, Madhusudan. He was the firstborn in our next generation. He fought and died for us.'

Feeling Krishna's eyes on him, Arjun meets them with his own. I was a dead man, he thinks. As long as Karna had that weapon, I was in mortal danger. Madhusudan saved *my* life. But to call Ghatotkach an enemy of dharma…He glances sideways at his older brother.

Bheem's eyes are blank, as if he is staring into a void. Then, he looks away, mutters something below his breath and leaves the gathering abruptly. The others stare after him anxiously. Let him be, says Yudhisthir. He needs to be alone.

❖

The first rays of the sun strike his body spreadeagled across the battle field. Riding lightly on them is that final image of the battle, the one eluding him all this while. It is that moment when Karna had looked up straight at him, just seconds before releasing the weapon. The resolve in his eyes was crystal clear, but there was no cruelty in it, only infinite compassion for his target, and a deeper understanding than any Ghatotkach has encountered before. You and I, that look said. We are akin.

The pain, *this* pain, is now building into a silent scream within his body. Whatever he had felt before this was nothing. Once he heard Krishna say those words to the Pandavas—the same Krishna he had so eagerly accepted as his master and commander in battle—it was worse than any wound that had been inflicted on his body. His whole life had been one of exclusion. Of wanting to win the regard of his family, even though they'd had little to do with him. He had hoped to make them proud, to help and serve them, to win their respect on their terms. And now, when they were taking a moment to mourn his death, they had been told instead to celebrate it. For, in the eyes of someone else, he was not worthy of being allowed to live. Everything he had believed in, had been told, had turned out a lie.

The agony reaches a crescendo. His eyes drift up to the sky. He does not look at any fixed spot. Above and around him, there is a growing darkness, sprinkled with tiny dots of light. Then, for the briefest of moments, the pain seems to disappear. His mouth is filled with a powerful force. What is it—a flood of emotion or his own blood? It does not really matter. He is free of everything that he had chased after, and that had spurned him. The blankness reaches out to catch him as he falls. It embraces him, as his mother first welcomed him, into this world. As he sinks into its comfort, he closes his eyes in relief. Nothing else can touch him now. Neither praise nor insult. He is free.

16

Reunion

The shadows are lengthening across the valley of the Bhagirathi. Perched lightly on a western peak in the Himalayas, the setting sun drizzles its light across the snows. The wind whips up powdery drifts chasing them down the slopes. Hidimbi stands on a rocky outcrop with the scene spread out beneath, a bird's eye view.

The women on the riverbank hold her attention. They have arrived a little earlier, driven up in chariots that wait some distance away. Together they walk to the river's edge and step in its sacred waters for a quick ritual bath. There are over a hundred of them, but they hardly make a sound. They are the women whose men were slaughtered at Kurukshetra. Nearly all are widows. Many have lost every close male relative: father, brothers, husband, sons. There are queens among them, but hard to say who is one and who is not. Who young, who old? They look as if they have all been handed out identical masks, the same austere grief twists everyone's face, the same silent prayers fall from their lips, the same humanity weighs down on their tired shoulders. Like her, they have all lost someone deeply loved. The thought that had been running through her head runs in them too, like a dirge that refuses to die: where are you now? If only I could see you just once. Where, O, where are you?

Scanning the women, she recognises one and stiffens in shock. Older now, but that stark face is unmistakable, the straight-backed posture too. She can only be Mata Kunti. However, there is something else about her that wasn't there before, a gauntness, as if a fire is burning her away from within. A woman who too is in torment.

Rancour, like acid, dissolves the sutures of Hidimbi's wounds. *Why is she here? Whom did she lose?* She recalls everything she'd learned about Ghatotkach's death. Karna had killed him. And then, two days later, he too was killed. Karna was a friend of Vrikodar's enemy, Duryodhan. He was also, it turned out, Mata Kunti's eldest son, born out of wedlock; a dirty secret that she'd kept hidden from everyone's sight, till the end. She would have had her motives for keeping quiet, thinks Hidimbi, sourly. Among all the women sitting on the riverbank, she perhaps was the only one who had gained something. Hadn't she got what she wanted? Hadn't her sons won back her husband's kingdom?

Bitterness rises in her, but just as suddenly it falls. I'm tired. I wish I could be different: indifferent. Grief has stripped me of everything, yet the longing remains. If only I could see my son once more, I would know peace. Stillness.

As if disapproving of her thoughts, the wind picks up. A whinging wind, it pulls at her hair, tugs at her ankles. Down in the valley, it is not as cold as up here, but not for long. The sun is lowering itself. What are the women waiting for?

'I knew that I'd find you here,' he says.

Her heart misses a beat and then starts thumping wildly. She becomes still. In her version of their story, it had always been love at first glimpse—something fated. But what was his version? Incidental lovers, he'd called them, suggesting that there was no *story* there, or nothing of any real significance. But still it had extracted from her an insufferable price. Maybe, from him too. There are changes, she notes, deeper furrows on his brow, a loss of brightness in his eyes, a droop around his mouth, stiffness from the long walk up the mountainside and, definitely, he suffers from a shortness of breath. The war, she concludes, seems to have diminished him. But she also can't help wondering: what does he see when he sees me?

Truce, his eyes tell her. The passion is gone. In its place is fatigue, a melancholy that has entered his bone marrow and slowed his zest for living. An appeal for understanding and forgiveness.

She is ready for everything, but not the last. My love meant nothing to you, my life was irrelevant. But not my son's life. *Why did you let him die?*

As if he has read her mind, a spasm crosses his face.

'Why are you here?' she asks coldly.

'Mahamuni Vyasa has said that there is to be a vision at dusk. It will heal...our pain.' He looks at her diffidently. 'I think we share that, don't we? We both need that healing.'

'We?' She frowns. 'You mean you and all those people who have come with you. Yes, I can understand the pain of those women, but yours?' She shakes her head slowly from side to side.

'Hidimbi, he was my son too.' He passes a hand over his face, as if erasing what he has allowed himself to feel before her. Those eyes of hers boring into him are unrelenting. 'Mothers lament their dead sons openly, but I, a father, must hide my grief. Just as I had to hide my love for him. If there was anyone who would understand, I hoped that person would be you.'

'What do you expect me to understand, Vrikodar? The part of my son that was me or the part of him that was you? The two are irreconcilable, you know that. My love was true but yours was just part of a larger scheme. His courage was true, but his death too was a set-up. No, don't shake your head like that. Don't bother to deny it…He dreamed of helping his father's side, but he was nothing more than a bait. At least, he served that purpose well, didn't he?'

'You don't—

'*Understand*?' she snaps.

'No. That wasn't what I was going to say.'

'Then?'

His eyes wander, as if looking for something. Suddenly, he points to the river bank. 'There! See that.'

The sun has slipped behind the western skyline. She sees a tall, dark man with a white beard enter the water. Mahamuni Veda Vyasa offers prayers silently. The river becomes still. Slowly a hum begins, dull at first, but rising, resounding all through the valley. The water turns a deep carmine, a vast blood stream again, a mother. Giant waves rise from her womb. The hum turns into a tumultuous roar. And the dead rise again in a cohort. All those who died at Kurukshetra, the armies of this earth that fought and killed each other, are a united legion in veeraswarga, the heroes' heaven. A fellowship of men wearing celestial robes and dazzling earrings, arm in arm. Laughing. Around them, weapons, chariots, steeds, elephants, shields and maces all part of the pageant. All aglow.

'Mahamuni Veda Vyasa promised that he would raise them,' says Vrikodar. 'And here they are. *Alive,* see!' He begins to name them for her: 'Pitamaha, Acharya Drona, Virat, Dhrupad, Drishtadyumna, Bhurishravas, Shalya, Bahlika, Somdatt...Oh! Duryodhan too...And next to him, Karna...There are the Draupadeyas, Subhadra's son Abhimanyu. And—'

She sees him at the same moment that he looks at her. Can it be? Oh, the joy! He is alive, my son lives.

A proud smile lights up his face. *Here I am, Mother. Among the champions.*

I can see that...It wasn't all for nothing then. Strange, how dying has given you the respect that life denied.

He throws back his head and laughs. *And even more strange, see how it has brought Hidimbi and Bheem together again.*

Yes, we have gained value due to your immortality. We have finally become a story. But losing you dwarfs every meaning.

You are my parents. I am what I set out to be—your son. That is meaning enough for me.

The waves are subsiding. The river returns to itself. The vision too dissolves. Yet, for a long time they stand there, seeing him that way.

Serene. Enlightened. Complete. Back in No-Time.

ALSO IN SPEAKING TIGER

THE KAUNTEYAS

QUEEN KUNTI'S MAHABHARATA

Madhavi Mahadevan

India's greatest epic retold from the point of view of Kunti, mother of the Pandavas and the tragic warrior Karna.

With a split destiny ruling her life, Kunti, given away at birth, leads a hard but uneventful existence in her foster-father's home. At fourteen she is pressed into the service of the temperamental sage Durvasa who grants her a boon. Its first use, however, only brings her adversity and a shameful secret.

With her marriage to Pandu, Kunti dreams of a better future, but a curse makes him leave the throne of Hastinapur to his sibling, the blind Dhritarashtra, and retreat to the forest. When Pandu dies suddenly, Kunti journeys back to the kingdom, no longer its queen but a widow; a dependant, as are her five sons. She must now take up the task of guiding them through the long struggle to get their inheritance, a struggle made harder by the discovery that Karna, the illegitimate child she had abandoned long ago, is alive and a sworn enemy of the Pandavas.

Recasting the *Mahabharata* from the viewpoint of Kunti, *The Kaunteyas* replaces the idealized mother figure with a fully three-dimensional woman, providing new insights into the epic.

ALSO IN SPEAKING TIGER

BRIDE OF THE FOREST

THE UNTOLD STORY OF YAYATI'S DAUGHTER

Madhavi Mahadevan

'A lush, wondrous reclaiming that rightfully centres a long-neglected character in the Mahabharata: Drishadvati aka Madhavi. A rich, pitch-perfect novel.' —Ashok Banker

The myth of Drishadvati appears in the *Mahabharata* as the 'story of the salvation of kings by a maiden.' While tales of surrogacy abound in the Indian epics, this is the first known example of a womb-on-rent. This strange story—of a girl whose fertility was bartered repeatedly in exchange for priceless horses—has intrigued modern scholars, playwrights and authors for its cultural significance. While earlier adaptations have cast its theme as the exploitation of a helpless woman, *Bride of the Forest* presents it as the story of girl who is surprisingly radical in her ultimate rejection of patriarchy.

Staying true to the original myths and springing entirely from the world of the *Mahabharata*, the novel brings to life several other characters: Garuda, the divine bird who flies Lord Vishnu around the world: the proud kings of Ayodhya, Pratisthan and Kashi; the arrogant queen, Devayani, and her duplicitous maid—whose stories reveal an intricate tapestry of human and divine relationships. Intertwined in the tales of traditional rivalries is the age-old war between the asuras and the devas that gave rise to the perennial male quest for immortality, transmuted into the human desire for sons that lies at the root of commercial surrogacy even today. However, it is the story of Drishadvati, her sacrifice and her nobility, that will enchant the reader.